Women's Liberation: Jesus Style

Edited by Stephanie Bibb

MESSAGES OF

SPIRITUALITY &

WISDOM FOR

TODAY'S

WOMAN

Contents

Contributors   1

Introduction   5

I. The Battle for Self-Esteem   11
My Friend Sam
by Rev. Brenda Salter McNeil

II. Coping With Grief and Pain   25
Family Focus on a Friday Afternoon
by Rev. Brenda J. Little

III. Building Relationships That Endure   37
Love That Goes the Distance
by Rev. Barbara A. Heard

IV. Never Ever Give Up   55
Pressing for My Blessing
by Dr. Vashti M. McKenzie

V. The Workplace Blues   71
Women's Liberation: Jesus Style
by Dr. J. Alfred Smith, Sr.

VI. My Sister, Myself   79
That Was Then . . . This Is Now
by Rev. Marsha Thomas

VII. It's Time to Make a Change   93
Breaking Free from the Waiting to Exhale Syndrome
by Dr. Jeanne L. Porter

VIII. Taming a Wild Woman   117
Jesus Made the Difference
by Dr. Jeremiah A. Wright, Jr.

More Liberating Sermons??   137

End Notes and Epigraph Sources   138

Dedicated to my family, whose love and encouragement continues to propel me forward, and to my friend, Dr. Colleen Birchett, who first recognized and called out the gift that lay within me.

Contributors

Rev. Barbara A. Heard is an associate pastor at Trinity United Church of Christ in Chicago, IL where she serves as pastoral liaison for women's ministries. Her ministry also includes teaching in the church's Center for African Biblical Studies and pastoral counseling. Rev. Heard was called to the ministry after twenty-five years of teaching in the Chicago Public School system. She is a graduate of Garrett-Evangelical Theological Seminary and was a recipient of the *Dr. & Mrs. Edgar Faust Preaching Award.*

Rev. Brenda J. Little is pastor of Bethany Baptist Church of Christ in Evanston, IL. Prior to assuming Bethany's pastorate, she served as co-pastor of Christian Church-Baptist in Chicago, IL, as assistant pastor of Second Baptist Church in Evanston, IL, and Protestant chaplain at Chicago's Westside Veteran's Administration Hospital. She has received numerous honors and awards, including the "Outstanding Woman of Evanston, IL" award from the NAACP in 1983. Rev. Little holds degrees from the Northern Baptist Theological Seminary, the Chicago Baptist Institute, and the Michael Reese Hospital Medical School of Nursing.

Dr. Vashti M. McKenzie is an ordained Itinerant Elder in the African Methodist Episcopal Church and pastor of Payne Memorial A.M.E. church in Baltimore, MD. Under her leadership, the church's congregation has tripled in size. Dr. McKenzie has been honored as a religious role model by many organizations, including 100 Black Women and Operation PUSH. She is national chaplain for Delta Sigma Theta Sorority and author of *Not Without A Struggle,* now in its fourth printing. She was also recognized by *Ebony Magazine* as one of America's fifteen greatest black women preachers in 1997. Dr. McKenzie holds degrees from United Theological Seminary, Howard University, and the University of Maryland.

Rev. Brenda Salter McNeil is an ordained Christian minister, teacher, evangelist, and frequent speaker at churches, colleges and conferences nationwide. She is the founder and president of Overflow Ministries, Inc., a multi-ethnic organization devoted to evangelism, reconcilement, and inner-healing. She also serves on the staff of Chicago's Intervarsity Christian Fellowship where she prepares and directs training programs and seminars designed to empower participants to effectively engage in racial reconcilement and cross-cultural ministry. Rev. McNeil holds degrees from Fuller Theological Seminary and Rutgers University.

Dr. Jeanne L. Porter is an associate minister at the Apostolic Church of God in Chicago, IL. She is a popular retreat and seminar leader for women and has conducted workshops across the nation. She is involved in leadership development as it relates to spiritual growth, and has worked with religious, civic, and political leaders to provoke personal and organizational transformation. Dr. Porter is also the founder and director of TransPorter Communications, an organization devoted to transforming men and women through the word of God. She holds a Ph.D. from Ohio University and has also attended United Theological Seminary and Ohio State University. She has taught at DePaul University and in the African American Leadership Partnership Program at McCormick Theological Seminary, both located in Chicago, IL.

Dr. J. Alfred Smith, Sr. is senior pastor of Allen Temple Baptist Church in Oakland, California. Under his leadership, the church's congregation has grown from fewer than 1,000 members in 1970 to over 4,000 members today. He is also a professor at the American Baptist Seminary of the West. Dr. Smith was cited in 1993 by *Ebony Magazine* as one of America's top black preachers. He has received over 125 awards and published over sixteen books. Dr. Smith is a past president of the American Baptist Churches of the West and the Progressive National Baptist Convention. He holds degrees from Golden Gate Seminary, American Baptist Seminary of the West, the Missouri School of

Religion, and Western Baptist College.

Rev. Marsha Thomas is an ordained Christian minister and a graduate of the Chicago Theological Seminary. She served for five years as Minister of Pastoral Care at New Faith Baptist Church in Matteson, IL. In 1993, she founded Sister to Sister Ministries, an organization designed to provide counseling to women and their families in the areas of spiritual growth, self -esteem, relationships, and stress management.

Dr. Jeremiah A. Wright, Jr. is senior pastor of Trinity United Church of Christ in Chicago, IL., the largest and fastest grow- ing church within its denomination. Under his leadership, the church's congregation has grown from 87 members in 1971 to over 6,000 members today. Dr. Wright has co-men- tored two doctoral programs at United Theological Seminary and has published numerous books, including *Africans Who Shaped Our Faith* and *Good News! Sermons of Hope for the Family.* He holds degrees from Howard University, the University of Chicago Divinity School, and United Theological Seminary.

Introduction

Making it in the world with little money and no man. Building self-esteem. Establishing friendships. Constructing strong families. Coping with problems that have knocked you flat down. And just staying sane in a crazy world. These are issues with which many women are confronted on a daily basis. They are a part of our battle to survive. But what do these issues have to do with the Bible?

During his ministry, Jesus worked relentlessly and ultimately gave his life to empower and liberate all who were oppressed, including women. And since the beginning of time, God has used both women and men to illustrate God's undying love and concern for each of us. Many women, however, have a difficult time finding images in the Bible that reflect their uniquely feminine issues and emotional struggles, largely because the trials, quests, and triumphs of the Bible's women are not always easy to identify. Frequently, these stories are buried, like diamonds embedded beneath the earth. And like diamonds, they must be excavated—a mission that can be accomplished only through prayer, sensitivity, and insight.

This book contains the works of eight African American preachers who have done a superb job of digging deeply to find those precious gems. Within this book, you will find a volume of invigorating and liberating sermons consistent with an interpretation of the gospel that will change your perception of yourself and your role in this world.

Your spirit will find it refreshing to learn that the word of God provides supportive commentary concerning female bonding, sisterhood, and economic discrimination on the basis of gender—issues resurrected during contemporary times by the feminist/womanist movements. The notion of women relying upon other women for help in getting through life's more difficult life situations is portrayed in the Old Testament story of Ruth and Naomi, which is passionately recounted by Rev. Barbara Heard. Through the story of Sarai and Hagar, Rev. Marsha Thomas urges us to examine our treatment of other women and challenges us to broaden the reality of sisterhood in our lives. In addition, the present day reality of economic exploitation resulting from gender discrimination is examined through the prism of the Scripture by Dr. J. Alfred Smith, Sr.

The richest illustrations of God's intimate connection with women and their issues are found in the gospels of Matthew, Mark, Luke, and John. Jesus, who came to earth to set all captives free, talked openly and freely with women, telling them what they needed to do to get their acts together. In most cases, counsel given emphasized the need for liberation from internal bondage—those weaknesses in spirit or character that cause us to do damage to ourselves. Jesus encouraged the women of his day to identify and appropriate the dormant power within themselves in order to force change in external circumstances. Four biblical passages that recorded such exchanges between various women and Jesus Christ are masterfully recounted and analyzed by Rev. Brenda J. Little, Dr. Vashti McKenzie, Rev. Brenda Salter McNeil, and Dr. Jeremiah A. Wright, Jr.

During the 1990's, any book dealing with women's issues would be incomplete without acknowledging the impact of Terry McMillan's blockbuster novel, *Waiting to Exhale*, on current day popular thought. The novel and screenplay that followed ushered in an avalanche of commentary, both within and outside of the African American religious community. Dr. Jeanne Porter cuts through the hype to the essence of McMillan's message by connecting the behavioral issues exposed by McMillan to the teachings of Jesus on the very same topic many centuries ago.

Through these stories, God is showing women (and men, too!) a way out, a way through, and a way around the obstacles that threaten to steal our hopes and dreams for the present. The ability of each of the contributors to intermingle the liberating message of God's word with the everyday life issues we face is priceless. You will find God's word, as preached by those featured in this book, to be liberating, self-empowering, and providing strength for life's daily struggles. It certainly has done all of that for me—and much more. My purpose in compiling and editing this book is to share with you the transforming power of Jesus Christ as I have experienced it. With practical application of this book's contents to your everyday life, your internal power will flow and your greatest potential will be achieved!!

Chapter One:
The Battle for Self-Esteem

"Deal with yourself as an individual worthy of respect and make everybody else deal with you the same way."

Nikki Giovanni, poet and activist

※

Samantha was a woman who thought of herself as worthless. Others held a low opinion of her, and she held a low opinion of herself. Her past was littered with many mistakes—the consequences of her own futile attempts to convert herself into a "somebody," which added to her shame. But while doing routine chores one day, she encountered a man who taught her how to permanently quench her thirst and fill her deepest, most intimate needs. Discover how Samantha was able to regain her sense of dignity and worth. Perhaps her story can help you.

My Friend Sam

Rev. Brenda Salter McNeil

Scripture: John 4:1-42

This story is about a woman whose name we do not even know. She is called the Samaritan woman, and because I have come to know her so well and I have read through this story so many times, I decided to give her a name. I call her Samantha. So I would like to introduce you to my friend Samantha—Sam for short. As we read her story, we will probably find echoes of our own story laced within it.

Let me tell you some things about my friend Sam. She is a Samaritan, a woman who has grown up in a society that has discriminated against her on the basis of her race and gender. Perhaps you have an idea of what that feels like. Her society, first of all, has said she has been born of the wrong ethnicity. She is a Samaritan and because she has been born into this particular ethnic group, she has been ostracized and set side. All kinds of determinations, decisions, and prejudgments are made about her without anyone knowing anything about who she really is.

During the times in which Sam lived, Samaritans and Jews did not associate with one another.[1] In the Old Testament, God forbade the Israelites from intermarrying with other cultures because whenever they intermingled with other folks, the Israelites not only intermarried, but they also took on their gods and their customs. Therefore, God said, "You are separate and you are holy. You are mine, so you are not to entwine yourselves with other cultures or other gods. You are not to take on their pagan practices. Remember what happened to you when you got to Egypt? Since I know what you are prone to do, I want you to stay free and I want you to stay separated unto me when you get out of Egypt,"[2] said the Lord.

The Roots of Racial Prejudice

Later in their history, the Assyrians waged war upon the northern kingdom of the Israelites, captured them, and as a result intermarriage occurred. The offspring from those marriages were the Samaritans.[3] So every time any God-fearing, self-respecting Jew looked at a Samaritan, they were reminded of the sin, curse, and shame of having been invaded, conquered, and intertwined with another culture. As the years passed, prejudice grew and eventually the Jews began to refer to the Samaritans as half-breeds, and half-breeds eventually evolved into calling them dogs.

If you think of someone as a dog, you do not want to be around them. You do not want to be in the same temple with them. You do not want them in or close by your neighborhood. So, you give them a little section, some place where they can live. That is why no self-respecting Jew would be caught dead in Samaria or worshiping in the same temple with a Samaritan. The severity of Jewish prejudice against the Samaritans is what makes the story about the Good Samaritan so intriguing.

In that story, Jesus is traveling to Galilee, and the most direct way of getting there required passage through Samaria. But because most Jews would not be caught dead in that neighborhood, they developed an alternative route which required traveling on a curving road that circled a mountain. Curves in the road prevented travelers from seeing who was coming around the bend, which made it easy for people to be ambushed and robbed. The Good Samaritan helped a man who had been ambushed and hurt while traveling this circuitous route, known for its treachery and peril.

Understanding why a traveler chose this dangerous route illustrates the depth of the prejudice against the Samaritans, for the decision of the traveler tells us that he preferred to take his chances with robbers and thieves rather than journey through the neighborhood of "those ethnic people."

The Roots of Gender Discrimination

Not only was Samantha a Samaritan, which was one strike against her, but she was also a woman. Women in that culture were property. Women first belonged to their fathers and upon marriage they belonged to their husbands. As a female, your sole purpose in life was to bear children, preferably a lot of boys, since male children had greater worth in society than females.[4] That is why the prayers of Sarah,

Hannah, Elizabeth, and other biblical women who begged God for a child were so excruciating. This attitude was reflected in a prayer of God-fearing men of those times. They would enter the temple and say, "Lord, I thank you that I was not born a slave or a Gentile or a woman."[5]

Erosion of Self-Esteem

Can you imagine what this did to Sam's self-esteem and sense of worth? And if that were not enough, to be a Samaritan woman had an additional stigma attached to it. Somewhere along the line, the prejudice and hatred became so entrenched that people began to refer to Samaritan women as perpetual menstruators.

In the Old Testament, a woman was considered unclean during her menstrual cycle and set aside from her community until it was completed, at which time she would present herself for cleansing at the temple.[6] This tradition was rooted in the biblical teaching that the life of all flesh is within the blood, so if someone was bleeding, contact with their blood was self-defilement.[7]

Someone decided that Samaritan women were perpetual menstruators, which meant that from childhood until old age, there was never a day that a Jew would consider a Samaritan woman clean. There was never a day that a Jew would think a Samaritan woman was clean enough to sit on the same seat on which a Jew sat. Anything upon which a perpetual menstruator sat was burned or discarded.

Anything from which she drank was broken. No one else could eat after her because to do so would bring self-defilement.

Can you imagine being considered dirty 365 days of the year, every day of your life? This is the culture in which my friend Samantha grew up. Knowing all of this helps us to better understand her. I think Sam heard too many negative messages about herself. "You are no good." "You do not have worth." "You are not intelligent enough." These were negative messages Sam received since it was forbidden for a father to teach his daughter the law of God, the Torah.

An Unquenchable Thirst

Because many young girls are feisty, they might initially fight against those negative messages, but after hearing them over and over again, the messages begin to sink into their psyches and affect their self-esteem. I understand that over the years, my friend Sam developed a hole in her heart. She lacked nurturance and affirmation, and after a while, she began to thirst for somebody who would love, affirm, and validate her. I think that she had what I call an unquenchable thirst.

You and I may live in a culture that is not quite as extreme as Sam's, but as women, we are also frequently bombarded with negative messages and must continually fight to prevent those messages from seeping too deeply into our psyche.

A Hole In Our Hearts

Some of us have developed holes in our hearts. Perhaps you grew up in a home in which your parents unknowingly compared you with your brothers so much that your sense of being a female was lost. Perhaps in your family you were not the smartest or most articulate one. Perhaps because you were shy and quiet, and because your family did not understand who you really were, they unintentionally failed to nurture you. Or perhaps too many of the commercials carrying messages saying that women need to look like this and ought to be like that kept you in a constant state of feeling inadequate—not feeling quite beautiful enough. It is easy for women in any culture to develop a need for nurturance, affirmation and validation.

Perhaps English is not your first language, but in this country, assumptions concerning your intelligence, sophistication, and ability to negotiate the system are based upon the type of accent your voice reflects. Eventually you realize that people assume you can not do the job because of the way you speak or the way you look. I know how it feels to be in a profession with relatively few women. As a minister, every time I stand before a crowd, there is a part of me that needs to prove that I can do it. These types of situations create a thirst. If we examine ourselves, we might find that Samantha's story is a whole lot like our own.

Quenching Your Thirst In All of the Wrong Ways

Let me tell you how my friend Sam tried to quench her thirst; she sought romantic relationships. She was thirsty and in need of validation, nurturance, and affection. It is alright to seek nurturance, and it is normal to want affection and to sometimes need attention. But because Samantha never received any of these things, she became very thirsty. And maybe because we did not get all of these things, we are also a little thirsty.

I do not know how you are trying to quench your thirst, but Sam began to look for love in all the wrong places. She wanted to find someone who would affirm her, tell her she was pretty, and say to her, "You are important, you matter, there is nobody like you." So she attempted to fill this void, this vacuum, this hole by finding male friends who would say, "Oh, honey, there is nobody like you and I just can't wait to marry you. I want to love you! I want to spend my life with you! I want to marry you!" What validation! What affirmation! What nurturance!

While you may not be quenching your thirst in the way Sam did, there are many different means by which people seek to quench thirst. College students sometimes try to quench their thirst through academic achievement. They may have a real hole in their hearts and are attempting to fill it by getting straight A's, to boost their confidence. They shudder at the possibility of receiving anything less than an A because their sense of worth and self-esteem are riding on it.

Or it could be, that like Sam and me, you got married? We did not get affirmation from our parents at home, so we got married with the expectation of receiving it from our husbands. Or perhaps you said, "I can not get my husband to nurture, care, and affirm me so that the hole in my soul will be filled, so I'll have a baby." I know that feeling. I was completely engrossed in being a new mother. It felt so good just to look at that little face that loved me so.

Other people may use professional achievement, or a career-oriented lifestyle that demands extremely hard work, to quench their thirst. Maybe that is why we have the term "workaholics" in this society.

I do not know how you are quenching your thirst. For some, it could be a sexual liaison. There are some people who never expect to be blessed with a long-term relationship, so they decide to settle for a good time. Some use drugs or alcohol to fill a vacuum in their lives. Others use money; the more they spend the better and more secure they feel.

All of these behaviors come from the hearts of thirsty people. None of us grew up in homes with perfect parents because parents are not perfect. Although most do the best they can, parents are human and therefore make mistakes. So, on some level there is probably a little bit of thirst in all of us. And if society provokes the small hole that already exists in our souls, it expands and the thirst becomes greater.

The Insatiability of Sin

At this point, something should be noted about sin. It is totally insatiable. I do not believe that Sam woke up one morning and said, "Let me see how many times I can get married." I think each time she met a man, she hoped that he would be the one. The nature of sin is that it only provides temporary relief. It will feel good for a while, but it will always be temporary and you will get thirsty again. I do not think most people engage in sexual relationships because they feel like having one encounter after another. Rather, I think they are thirsty and after a while, their thirst needs to be quenched again. I think that whatever means we choose to try to satisfy our thirst will always be temporary and Jesus wants to bring that to our attention.

Perhaps you have three children but that still has not filled the void completely. You are married now, but that is not doing it. You earn a salary larger than you ever imagined, but that still does not do it. You are driving one luxury car while a second one sits at home in the garage, but you still are not satisfied. You purchased a house, but now you want a larger one. There is something about this world that makes people feel a need to keep being satisfied over and over again.

Understanding all of this, Jesus says to Sam, "I know you have been married five times, and you are in another relationship right now because this is the only way you can think of to quench your thirst. But you are not even married to him."[8] In response, Sam does what most of us do when Jesus puts his finger smack dab on our most personal issue and deepest need—she evaded him by changing the subject!

Thirst No More

This is when the wrestling with God begins. Jesus says to Sam in verse 14 of our Scripture, "Just know that if you keep trying to do it your way and through the means that come to your own mind, you will keep getting thirsty over and over again, but whoever drinks the water I give will never thirst again." You must come to the conclusion that what you are really looking for can only be found in God, and for many that will cause a struggle.

My friend Sam has reached the conclusion that what she is looking for can not be found in a sixth husband. She could get married seventeen different times and still become thirsty again. It is not in a new hairstyle, it is not about becoming prettier, and it is not about losing weight. Although God does want us to have sound bodies and good health, the answers we seek do not lie in these things. What we are really looking for can be found only in God. So get the new house, the new car, the education or whatever it is that you want. Just understand that when it is all said and done, the hole in your heart can only be filled by God. I can not speak for you, but I have had a hard time reaching this conclusion. Each of us must wrestle with God before reaching the point where we give up and say, "Alright, God, I will do it your way. I have tried every trick in the book. I have done everything I know to do. I give up. What do you want me to do? Show me your way."

Gaining an Internal Resource

Jesus said to Sam, "I am He, the one who can permanently quench your thirst. If you take a drink of this Living Water, I will give you an internal resource. I will place a spring within you."[9]

Everything my friend Sam has done to this point has been externally driven. She has hoped that this person might have it or that person might have it, but Jesus said, "You can stop looking outside of yourself. Instead, I am going to put something inside of you so that you will not have to look any further than within yourself to begin to satisfy your thirst."[10]

So I welcome you to the well. Welcome to the place where Jesus pulls up a chair, sits down, has a personal conversation with you, and puts his finger smack dab on your most piercing issue—without destroying your self-esteem, stripping away your dignity, or taking away your freedom to choose. He simply says, "If you are really tired of being thirsty, and if you do not want to keep coming here to draw water, then why don't you let me satisfy your thirst?"[11]

Meditation and Prayer

Lord, help me day by day to obliterate any negative messages to which I am overtly or subtly exposed with the force that flows from your never ending love for me. Reveal to me my deepest longings, and by your grace, show me how to fulfill those longings in positive and self-affirming ways so that I will thirst no more. I thank you in advance for filling my void without taking away my dignity or freedom to choose.

Chapter Two:
Coping With Pain and Grief

"Ah done been in sorrow's kitchen and ah licked de pots clean."

Gullah proverb

We live in a violent world. Cruel, uncontrollable, and destructive forces often heave devastating physical and emotional pain upon those who least deserve it. How do you prevent yourself from unraveling under the weight of the grief evoked by the violent death of a loved one? How do you deal with the psychological trauma that accompanies feelings of loss, abandonment, disappointment, and humiliation?

As a result of the group counseling session conducted at the foot of a cross one Friday afternoon, a grieving mother was equipped with what she needed to cope with one of the most devastating emotional crises any parent can experience—the loss of a child. Perhaps the wisdom and healing dispensed during that counseling session can help to soothe some your emotional bruises.

Family Focus On A Friday Afternoon
Rev. Brenda J. Little

Scripture: John 19: 25-27

Families have been receiving much attention in the media during recent presidential elections. Families have been receiving much publicity in books, news articles, magazines, seminars, and conferences. The disciplines of sociology and psychology have been doing more and more research in the area of family dynamics, family therapy, and family conflict in the last decade. And rightfully so, because we are living in a time when we see many families falling apart at the seams. The move now is to rebuild the strong families we say we once had, and the cry is for families to unite; for families to get together. We have even coined a modern term describing family interaction. We say that families need 'quality time' together, meaning that when families are able to spend time together, they ought to make the best possible use of it. Families are admonished to communicate with one another, to dialogue with one another, and to bond with one another.

Family Dynamics

It is strange how we do not view families as valuable until we find ourselves about to lose them, when we have to attend a funeral, or when we find ourselves in a crisis situation. And if you really want to study some interesting family dynamics, try observing the dynamics of a family situation when death has occurred. Some strange family dynamics surround the death of a family member. Some of you know what I am talking about. We come out of some strange bags when a loved one dies. It does not have to be anyone close to us. It can be third or fourth generation cousins, but suddenly everybody shows up out of the woodwork. Some strange family dynamics can be observed during death.

The Concern of Jesus for His Family

This emphasis on family relationships brings me to the foot of the cross where John records the words of Jesus. Jesus first says to his mother, "Woman, behold thy son."[1] He then turns to his beloved disciple and says, "Behold thy mother,"[2] or "Here is your mother." Crisis counseling was carried out from the cross during an era that preceded today's relationship seminars and the practice of family therapy. Before the word "bonding" was popularized and used as a therapeutic term thrown around in psychological circles, Jesus took time out of excruciating pain and death on an old rugged cross to reverse his role.

Jesus' Core Group

As he hung there looking out at his mother, Jesus took on the role of a group facilitator from the cross. Only a small group was there at the foot of the cross, and notice that all of the gospels let us know as a matter of record that it was the women who held vigil at Jesus' death. So, it is not surprising that the group encounter included Mary, the mother of Jesus, Mary Magdalene, Jesus' aunt, and the beloved disciple, John. This was the core group that chose to remain during the final hours.

You know, you may have a lot of friends, acquaintances and folk who come around when times are good, but there is a core group that continues to stick around in adverse circumstances. When things are going great, you can look up and see a large congregation, with many folks flocking around you. But when the going gets rough, the crowd starts to dwindle. I see a core group who chose to remain in that final hour at the foot of the cross, and they were dealing with some heavy stuff.

The Pain of Desertion

The issues confronting the core group were by no means lightweight. Jesus was suffering excruciating physical pain, but in addition to his physical suffering there was another kind of pain. Jesus was also suffering emotional pain, the kind of pain that comes when your heart has been broken. Where were his disciples? Where were his buddies? Where were the companions? Where were the good church members? Where were the loyal and faithful? When you look around and you do not see those that have been close to you when times were good, it causes a pain like none other inside of your heart. Jesus realized that part of his support group was missing—only a very small portion of his original support group was there.

However, a core group remained, consisting of his mother, his faithful follower Mary Magdalene, his aunt, and the disciple whom he loved, who tradition has identified as John. They remained, standing close enough to hear the words of Jesus. The gospel writer tells us that Jesus looked from the cross and as his body sagged against the weight of the nail, he had to perhaps lift himself up just a little bit in order to catch a breath of air. He needed enough air in his lungs to allow his diaphragm to move, so that he would be able to give out the words that he needed to express.

Jesus Deals with the Emotional Stress of Motherhood

Through his agony, Jesus focused his attention on his mother Mary—the one who had nursed him at her breast, the one who had cradled him in her arms, the one who had bought his first pair of school shoes, the one who had fed him, the one who sent him off to Sunday School for the first time. He looked at her approaching the age of fifty, which was considered old during those times, wondering what would happen to her. We do not know where his four brothers and two sisters were. Tradition says his father Joseph was dead. However, his mother was there, and Jesus took time out of dying to be concerned about her welfare. His mother was standing beneath him, choking back the tears, watching him hanging there, wondering in her mind what was going on, and asking, "Why don't you come down, son? You raised Lazarus from the dead. You made the lame to walk and the dumb to talk. You opened the eyes of the blind. You spoke and the elements stood at attention. You cooled fevers. So why, son, don't you come down? You know I'm a widow and I'm going to be left alone."

But I also see the Primary Counselor in this situation looking out in a sensitive way, using his sensitivity to facilitate his session with very few words. Because time was running out, Jesus used as few words as possible. Although the words he selected were few in number, they were very powerful because he was dealing with some powerful stuff in this encounter group. The issues included separation, greed, death, guilt, hurt, pain, helplessness, hopelessness, anguish, and anger. Because he was trying to deal with them all at the same time, Jesus had to be selective about his words.

That is something that we can learn from Jesus as pastors, preachers, counselors, and group facilitators. When counseling, sometimes we need to use as few words as possible. We need to extend our antennas and become sensitive to the needs of the people, while asking God for the discerning spirit of the Holy Ghost, in order to perceive what is going on in the hearts and minds of those being counseled.

There was a lot to deal with in this one group encounter, but Jesus continued to act as Primary Counselor, despite his indescribable pain. When speaking to his mother, Jesus addressed her as woman. Do you understand the significance of that? The term "woman" is not as emotional as the term of "Mama" or "Muth'Dear" or "Mommy" or "Mom" or "Ma." He selected a term that was less emotional because his sensitivity helped him to realize that Mary was already struggling. She was on the verge of falling apart, seeing her son on the cross bleeding and his life almost ready to come to an end. Mary was experiencing one of the strongest emotions that can touch a woman—the emotions that are evoked when your child calls you Mother, when your child cries out Mama, especially when he or she is hurting. The strength of this emotion can tear the insides of your heart apart, so I imagine that Mary was on the verge of collapse. A sensitive primary counselor picks up on these little things that become significant in a support group.

Jesus then reversed his approach by using emotional words when addressing John. Jesus says to him, "Behold thy mother", or "See your mother." Jesus is saying to John, "I'm changing your role now, and you're going to take on a new obligation. You are going to become Mary's son, and this is your mother." He wanted John to remember that from this time on, he had a new responsibility. Jesus placed his mother in the best care available. We know this because John was the only disciple that thought and cared enough to be there at the foot of the cross. Jesus knew he could depend on John. Mary needed love, understanding, and support now, and she would feel quite at home in her nephew's house. Although the words spoken to this group at the foot of the cross were few, they were therapeutic and powerful enough to let us know that crisis counseling had taken place.

Jesus Soothes Emotional Pain

Each member of that small group was helped at the cross because Jesus, although suffering, remained sensitive. When you are hurting, you need a sensitive person to deal with the hurt. You do not need any excess baggage. You do not need any excess conversation. You do not need any rap and you do not need any unfocused talk. You need somebody who can come to the point and do it in an anointed, powerful way.

Just seeing those four people at the foot of the cross helped Jesus with his heartache. I am sure it felt good for Mary to know that she had some human shoulders upon which she could rely. It is good for folks to say they are going to pray for you when things go wrong in your life and for them to let you know that they are there for you when someone dies, but there's nothing better than feeling the human flesh of somebody who has made his shoulder available for you to lean on. Jesus' aunt and Mary Magdalene were helped with their sense of hopelessness and helplessness by knowing that they didn't have to be there at the foot of the cross all by themselves. It is good to know somebody else is feeling like you are and that you are not alone in your emotional struggles. It was therapeutic for John to receive these last instructions from his teacher and master.

It is evident that bonding occurred in this group encounter at the foot of the cross, long before the term "bonding" was defined or coined. In this encounter group, healing and caring took place. In this group, trust was established. A healthy kind of intimacy was experienced. Relationships were established in this group. A mother was provided for in this group. A friend and a brother were affirmed in this group. An auntie was consoled in this encounter group and a follower was given self-esteem in this encounter group. All of this was accomplished by a Savior suffering on a cross who served as group facilitator, counseling others as he was dying.

This is more family therapy than we will ever learn in a seminary. This is more family therapy than we will ever learn in a workshop. This is more family therapy than we will ever learn in a classroom. Out of this support group a new family of God was established, which was identified by love and trust. That is why I can not forget the family counseling session that occurred one Friday afternoon. It is the most effective one I have ever witnessed, and I did not have to pay $150.00 an hour to be able to sit in on it!

God Provides Us With A Support Group

This family counseling session should always remind us that God has made some provisions for us in our groups. In the new family of God, we can leave the cross with relationships intact, not broken. We can leave the cross with trust, not distrust. We can leave our counseling session with Jesus knowing that we will not have to go through hurt, suffering or separation all by ourselves. We can go through hurt if someone is with us. We can go through separation if someone is with us. We can go through suffering if someone is with us. We can go through pain if someone is with us.

I also like the counseling session at the foot of the cross because I learned that you need a support group. A while ago, I had to go to the hospital for surgery. On the way to the operating room, the nurse tried to tell my husband to move out of the way so she could do what she had to do. My husband turned to her and said, "We're in this as partners, and where she goes, I go. I am her support group and I will support her in the holding room, in the operating room, and in the sick room."

God will send you a support group. Yes he will, oh yes he will! God will send you a support group. "Be not dismayed, whatever be-tide, God will take care of you and you and you."[3] I am glad about it! I am glad about that crisis counseling that took place at the foot of the cross. Thank you, Jesus! Thank you, Jesus! Thank you, Jesus!

Mediation and Prayer

God, help me to come to grips with my pain. I understand that at different times I hurt in different ways for different reasons. Sometimes the pain is physical and at other times it is emotional. Regardless of its form, I must realize that pain is usually a wake up call, alerting me that an immediate change is needed in order to propel myself towards a more peaceful reality.

Grief flowing from death of a loved one signals me that I must bring that relationship to closure. At other times, my hurt forces an abrupt acknowledgment that I have placed myself in a situation or done something that is not good for me. Lord, although my heart is aching, help me find within myself the courage and strength to move on, thereby initiating the process of healing. And Lord, thank you for your generous overflow of love—a soothing, gentle balm that eases this process of self-restoration.

Chapter Three: Building Relationships That Endure

"I don't believe that the accident of birth makes people sisters or brothers. It makes them siblings. Gives them mutuality of parentage. Sisterhood and brotherhood is a condition people have to work at."

Dr. Maya Angelou, poet and writer

No one can make it in this world alone. Everybody needs a support system—biological, adopted, or extended family members to whom we know we can turn to for love, encouragement, and help when we need it. But have you ever noticed that while adversity seems to strengthen the bonds of some families, it causes an irreparable rupture within others? Why are some support systems able to endure for a lifetime while others prematurely weaken and fall apart, leaving us feeling isolated and alone? Let two women who learned the secret of building a family support system that endures pass their wisdom on to you.

Love That Goes the Distance

Rev. Barbara A. Heard

Scripture: Ruth 1:1-19

The book of Ruth focuses on a single family. The story underscores the loyalty and fidelity that binds a family together. Families come in many sizes and configurations. Society says that a wife, a husband, and 2.5 children comprise the ideal family. Sometimes the house in the suburbs with a yard and a white picket fence is thrown into the picture for good measure.

Throughout the Scripture, there are stories about families, some of which are strange, weird, and bizarre. Many of those biblical families would be labeled dysfunctional by today's psychologists and social workers, but when studied carefully, they help us to realize that there is nothing new under the sun. From the beginning, back in Genesis, we observed the first triangular relationship between a husband named Abraham, a wife named Sarah, and a mistress named Hagar.[1] Abraham also had a nephew named Lot, whom I have always had serious difficulty understanding. What kind of man and father was this character named Lot to offer his own daughters to the men in the town of Sodom for sexual relations?

I find it hard to understand a father who would willingly and without hesitation offer his daughters for promiscuous sex.[2]

Later the writer of Genesis tells us that because of jealousy and envy within a family, Joseph's brothers sold him into slavery.[3] In the eleventh chapter of Judges, we find the story of Jephthah and his daughter, who unfortunately, like Lot's daughters, has no name. She's merely known as Jephthah's daughter. Jephthah's ambition and longing for power and prestige motivated him to promise a sacrificial offering to God, but his promise turned into a horrible nightmare that resulted in the death of his daughter. A daughter's love for her father turned her into a victim of a man's foolish ego. In the tenth chapter of the New Testament Gospel of Luke, we find a family comprised of two sisters named Mary and Martha and their brother, Lazarus. No mention is made of their parents, nor do we know if they had spouses, but the three of them comprised a family nonetheless.

Families come in many different sizes and configurations. Some families are strange and some family members are strange. Yet, we do not choose our families. Families come ready made. We are born into a family. We inherit a family, like it or not. Like a marriage, families are ours for better or for worse and until death do us part. Some of us have families who have rejected us. Years ago it was the teenage, pregnant girl who was thrown out of the home or ostracized from the church. Today it is the persons with HIV/AIDS who risk estrangement and alienation from family, friends, and the church. It seems that HIV/AIDS is the modern day version of the leprosy seen during the time in which Jesus lived. During those days, lepers were set apart, marginalized, despised, rejected, and considered unclean. How similar that is to our attitude and behavior toward persons living with AIDS! Some of us have families who have rejected us because of our sexual preference and our lifestyle. I have family members who do not understand my commitment to the church. And even Jesus' family was not sure about him or his lifestyle. After all, he ran around with some very questionable characters like prostitutes, tax collectors, wine bibbers, and smelly fishermen.

The church is still not the safe, loving place that God has called it to be. Some of us know people who have been asked to leave a church or have been made to feel very unwelcome in the church for the very reasons just stated. Yet, I wonder how many sexually abusive men have been asked to leave their homes or their churches? How many wife batterers does the church refuse to allow to enter its doors on Sunday morning? That is why I praise God for the promise he has given us, for God has promised in his word that when mother or father forsakes you, then he will take you up. "What a friend we have in Jesus, all our sins and grief to bear!"[4]

Once when Jesus was busy speaking to a big crowd, someone told him that his mother and brothers were waiting to speak to him. Jesus replied, "Who is my mother? Who are my brothers? Whoever does the will of my Father in heaven is my brother, sister and mother."[5] Then Jesus pointed to his disciples and said, "Here are my mother and my brothers."[6] These words spoken by Jesus reflect the reality of the popular saying "friends are the family we choose for ourselves."

The Extended Family

And so it was with Jesus. He seldom had the luxury of being around his biological family. He had parents and siblings, but even at twelve years of age Jesus was found sitting with the leaders of the temple, tending to his Heavenly Father's business. Throughout the gospels, we witness the disciples acting as both the family and friends of Jesus. In other words, Jesus had an extended family.

Families in any context, whether it is a church family, a biological family, an adopted family, friends, or an extended family, may include persons known as fictive kin. Andrew Billingsley, in his book *Climbing Jacob's Ladder*, makes reference to fictive kin. Billingsley uses this term to describe the component of the African American family consisting of persons unrelated by blood. We call them our play mothers and fathers, play sisters and brothers, play aunts, uncles, and cousins. According to Billingsley, this concept of fictive kin has a strong basis for family unity in the African American community.[7] In the African American community, many of us grew up with so many of these play aunts, uncles and cousins that they became an integral part of our lives, to the extent that we could hardly separate the play relatives from the real ones. This was certainly true for my daughter, Holly, whose childhood was filled with play aunts, play uncles, and play cousins who continue to perform a major role in her life as an adult.

In his book, Billingsley asserts that people can simply decide to live and act toward each other as family. As a child, I never heard of homeless people. People without families or with no place to call home were absorbed into someone's home and treated like family. A colleague once told me of a cousin who had been a part of her family as long as she could remember. Many years passed before she learned that this man was not a blood relative but someone her mother had taken in because he had nowhere to go.

Families come in many sizes, many configurations, and a variety of contexts. The story of Ruth centers around a family of three: a mother-in-law named Naomi and her two daughters-in-law named Ruth and Orpah. This story tells us of three widows whose husbands were dead and gone from their lives, three women bound together in love, bound together by friendship, bound together by family ties, and bound together by the blood of Christ. They were not a perfect family by societal definition, but they were a family nonetheless. What had begun as a family of six had been reduced by death to a family of three. And because there were no sons or husbands, the women seemingly had nothing to live for.

Naomi wanted to return home to Bethlehem, so she suggested that her two daughters-in-law return home to their respective families, also. Naomi reasoned that back at home among their own people, Ruth and Orpah would have a better chance of finding husbands and beginning new lives. In her bitterness and disillusionment, Naomi felt that she no longer had anything to offer them. Even if her husband had still been alive, she was too old to have more sons. Naomi felt tired and defeated and was convinced that God had dealt her a bitter cup in this distant land of Moab. So now, all she wanted to do was to return to the homeland she had been forced to leave years earlier because of famine. Once again, thanks be to God, there was food in her land, so she decided that it was time to go home again.

Going Home Again?

Like Naomi, some of us may have reached an impasse or encountered a crisis that turned our lives around or upside down. During that time we may have heard someone say that, "home is a place that when you go there they have to take you in." While that may be a comforting thought for some, there are others who may not want to be taken in. Sometimes we may choose not to go home again. Maybe there is some serious reason why we can not go back home. There may be some unresolved sibling rivalry or an abusive parent back home, so we choose to stay where we are and seek alternative solutions.

The three women in our story departed for Naomi's

homeland of Bethlehem, but halfway there, Naomi had a change of heart. She suddenly changed her mind about taking her daughters-in-law with her. Why make these young women leave their present home, a familiar place, to go to a new, unknown territory? Foreigners were not always welcomed by the Israelites so Orpah and Ruth may not fare so well there. Full of the wisdom that comes with age, Naomi gave her daughters-in-law all of the practical reasons why they should not follow her.

Unbreakable Ties

The idea of separating from each other filled these three women with such sadness that each wept bitterly. In the end Orpah, with a parting kiss, turned her heart toward home, but Ruth did not. Naomi's pleading did not prevail upon Ruth. As far as Ruth was concerned, all of Naomi's words were a wasted effort, going into one ear and out the other. No matter what her mother-in-law said, Ruth would not be moved. Ruth loved Naomi with a tenacity that went beyond geographic boundaries. It was a love bound so tightly by family ties that it would not allow her to leave her mother-in-law. They had come too far together and had been through too many things together to separate now. For Ruth, there was no turning back, so she clung to her mother-in-law and refused to leave her. From the depths of the heart, she spoke some of the most memorable words in the Old Testament: "Do not press me to leave you or turn back from following you. Where you go, I will go. Where you lodge, I will lodge. Your people shall be my people and your God, my God. Where you die, I will die. There I will be buried. May the Lord do thus and so to me and more as well, if even death parts me from you."[8]

The Marks of a Solid Relationship

Over the years of being together, time had built a solid foundation of mutual respect, friendship, love, and commitment between these two women. Such foundations are not easily uprooted by tragedy or sorrow and remain firm and solid, not easily disrupted by the changes that accompany every day living. How easily our family relationships can fall apart unless they are built on a solid foundation, not a foundation of material things—material things that are here today and gone tomorrow—or better yet, here today and gone today, if some burglar should gain entry into your home! In Ruth's famous and most wonderful words, we find expressions of unconditional love, devotion, faithfulness, acceptance, friendship, and commitment, all of which are necessary ingredients for a life-giving and life-affirming relationship between the members of any family, whether it is an adopted family, biological family, extended family, or those close friends who are the family we choose for ourselves. In the wonderful story of Ruth and Naomi, we find all the elements needed to sustain a meaningful and satisfying relationship, whether it is a relationship between men, a relationship between women, men and women, parent and child, or sister and brother.

Missing Pieces

Families come in many sizes and many configurations, but God honors commitment. God respects and honors loyalty between family members, regardless of the family size or the family context. God is looking for faithfulness, honesty, acceptance, and unconditional love within families and among family members.

As a minister, much of my time is devoted to counseling. I work with those who are about to be married, those who are already married, and those with relationships that are shaky. So many evenings I leave the church with a sad and grieved spirit because while I see many couples who are preparing to be married, I also see as many marriages that are on the verge of breaking up. In those marriages that are breaking up, I have noticed that there are some missing pieces. They remind me of a children's book I love entitled *The Missing Piece* by Shel Silverstein.[9] The intimacy that comes with self-disclosure is a missing piece and that hell-or-high-water type of commitment is a missing piece. Unconditional love, that kind of love that allows each partner to be who they are and to be accepted and appreciated for who God made them to be, is a missing piece. Open, honest communication is a missing piece. Acceptance of each other's imperfections is a missing piece.

Our God is relational and therefore created us to live in

relationships, but we have forgotten that we were created in God's own image. What image is that? God is love. God is patience, faithfulness, forgiveness, and acceptance. Paul gives you the whole list in the first book of Corinthians, chapter thirteen. Created in God's image, we are to exemplify these same characteristics in our family relationships. Some families have problems getting along because they have lost the image of God in their relationships and interactions with one another. There is no honesty, respect, love or commitment. It is as if they are not even family—the family ties seem nonexistent. Yet, if families are to remain in healthy, wholesome, and satisfying relationships, we must learn to disagree in an agreeable way. We must learn to speak the truth in love, and allow for our differences while appreciating the diversity each person brings to the table. If all of us were alike, just carbon copies of each other, this would indeed be a boring world!

Ruth knew that Naomi was old and embittered, but she never stopped loving or respecting her mother-in-law. Being left alone in Moab without any men to defend them put both women in a difficult and vulnerable position. This was especially true for Naomi since she was a foreigner with no family or traditional ties. In Old Testament times, a woman without a husband, sons, or even grandchildren had no status and was considered worthless. She was unable to provide for herself and could be easily preyed upon and victimized. Empty, bereft, and without hope, Naomi had no choice but to return home. Naomi tried hard to discourage her daughters-in-law from coming with her when she commanded, "Turn back, my daughters, go your way! Go home! Go back to your mother's house for the Lord has turned against me! Go back to your people and your gods! Do not follow after me!"[10]

Ruth saw her mother-in-law's despair and noticed her bitter complaint against God. Because she also felt Naomi's desolation, she decided to cast her lot alongside her mother-in-law. Out of love and commitment, Ruth chose to follow Naomi rather than return to the comfort and security of her parents' house in Moab. "Oh, blest be the tie that binds our hearts in Christian love!"[11]

Total Commitment

Ruth's decision is an illustration of the first and greatest commandment given by Jesus, which is to "love the Lord your God with all your heart, and with all your soul and with all your mind."[12] In this commandment, Jesus is demanding total commitment from us. Ruth understood this, for the words she spoke to her mother-in-law covered the entire gamut of life experience. The New American Bible puts it in a slightly different way. "Do not ask me to abandon or forsake you, for wherever you go, I'm going to go. Wherever you lodge, I will lodge. Your people shall be my people and your God my God. Wherever you die, I will die and there be buried. May the Lord do so and so to me and more besides, if aught but death separates me from you."[13] In other words,

Ruth was saying, "Let's get to the bottom line, girl. I am going where you go, I'm going to stay where you stay, and I'm going to die where you die. I'm even going to embrace your people and your God. There will be no leaving until death parts us."[14]

What more of a commitment could any of us ask for? With these words and actions, Ruth offered the depth of commitment that we see so little of in relationships today. Most of us have had fair-weather friends who hang around us when things are going well, when the money is flowing and the drinks are on the house. But let things start getting a little rough in our lives, let the rain begin to fall more frequently and somewhat harder than usual. Let the doctor diagnose us with cancer or discover that we are HIV positive. Then fair weather friends and family members disappear, sometimes never to be seen or heard from again, at least not when you need them. And if they do come around, it is to criticize and to make hurtful remarks that tear you down rather than encourage, support, and build you up.

Ruth's commitment to Naomi reminds me of a former coworker and her husband. During the early days of their marriage when they had their home built, her husband said, "I'm having an extra bedroom put downstairs so that when you get angry with me, you can go there until you cool off and if I get angry at you, I can sleep there. But there will be no leaving. We're in this thing together until death do us part." And, indeed, they were together until he died in 1967. Like Ruth, that husband believed in a committed relationship.

These are the kind of family ties that bind our hearts in Christian love. It has been said repeatedly that a family that prays together stays together. That may sound corny and trite to some, but I am suggesting that it takes a level of commitment that can only be ushered in by God to keep a family together. Ruth, through her willingness to embrace Naomi's God rather than the Moabite god, Chemosh, showed the depth of her commitment. Once Ruth committed herself to Naomi's God, the God of the Israelites, the God of Abraham, Isaac, and Jacob, there was no turning back.

Maya Angelou says it is because the black family has "banished the God of our ancestors, our children cannot pray."[15] God is love and because we no longer have him in our homes and our lives, we have forgotten how to love one another. Meanwhile, " . . . the adversary is within the gates, holding us up to the mirror of the world shouting, regard the loveless."[16] "We have forgotten," she says, "that we are more than keepers of our brothers and sisters. We are our brothers and sisters."[17] By placing God as the head of our family, no matter what difficulties we encounter, we have an anchor and a source of strength that will carry us through the Red Sea places in our lives and supply our needs during the time of famine—times when our marriages get shaky and our children act flaky—times when our homes seem to be coming apart at the seams, our money is scarce, and trouble seems to have moved in lock, stock, and barrel.

Like Naomi, we may also begin to question God and doubt God's credibility, but this story reminds us that God is faithful even when we are faithless. In this story of Ruth and Naomi, we witness a covenantal relationship between Naomi, Ruth, and God. We see God's desire for human relationships that goes beyond the call of duty. In the story of Ruth and Naomi, this kind of love is portrayed, recommended, and demonstrated as something that is attainable by humans. For we know that "with God all things are possible."[18]

Naomi and Ruth were blessed by family ties that bound them together. We too can experience the same blessings when we bind ourselves to Jesus Christ, ready to live in faithful commitment to God's will and God's way. As followers of Christ, we are bound together by the blood of the Lamb for "we have been bought with a price."[19] We are not our own, "but belong, body and soul, in life and in death to our Lord and Savior, Jesus Christ."[20] Just as Ruth's love for Naomi was unconditional, so is God's love for us unconditional. God, whose compassion is infinite, loves us with a love that will never let us go. Nothing, not even death, can separate us from God's love.[21]

Just as the story of Naomi and Ruth ends in joy and happiness, let me tell you my brothers and sisters, there is a blessing in this house waiting for you. There is joy, unspeakable joy and happiness beyond measure and it is all yours, when you accept the Lord Jesus Christ as your personal

Savior. If you are not experiencing joy in your relationships today, then come to Jesus. If there are some missing pieces in your life, come to Jesus. If you are in need of love and acceptance, come to Jesus. Give your heart, give your mind, give your soul and strength. Make a total commitment to the Lord Jesus Christ. The God of Naomi and Ruth wants to be your God, too. I dare you to try him!

Meditation and Prayer

Lord, I praise and thank you for those who loved and nurtured me from infancy into adulthood—be they biological, adopted, or extended family. Help my family to cultivate those qualities within our collective character that will strengthen us—unconditional love, respect, acceptance of and commitment to each other. We are trusting you to bind old wounds and heal old hurts that separate, and to help us fill in those missing pieces needed to fortify our relationships with each other. God, we invite you to entwine and enmesh yourself within our family ties, realizing that is the only way to ensure their endurance.

Chapter Four:
Never Ever Give Up

"When life knocks you down, try to fall on your back, because if you can look up, you can get up."

Les Brown

Lets face it—most of us have had days on which we would have preferred to remain in bed with our heads under the covers rather than arise to face the problems with which life was confronting us. Courageousness, perseverance and persistence are admirable virtues but on some days we just do not feel like putting them into practice.

When engaged in hand-to-hand combat with foreboding obstacles that threaten to kill, steal, and destroy your hopes and dreams, what course of action should you take? How do we gather and sustain enough strength to overcome our problems instead of allowing our problems to overcome us? How can an energy-sapping struggle be converted into a life-affirming one that leaves us being a better person for it? Learn the strategy behind successful struggle from a woman who successfully implemented that strategy and prevailed.

Pressing For My Blessing

Dr. Vashti M. McKenzie

Scripture: Matthew 15:21-28, Mark 7:24-30

Problems. I wonder if you know anything about problems? Problems are of the nature that if you have not had a problem, just keep living and you soon will. Problems are of the nature that you either have one now, you have just finished dealing with one, or there is a problem on the way.

Problems know exactly who you are. Your phone number may be unlisted, but problems have your name, your address, all of your telephone numbers, your beeper number, and your car phone number. Your problems will call you up, arrive unannounced at your front door, demand to come in, sit down at your dinner table, and expect to be fed. Problems do not have enough sensitivity to know when to go home. They will come back again the next night and demand your unsolicited attention. We have all had some problems in our lives. What is interesting to me is how we treat them. Often we look at our problems as another unfair act of God. Remember the time when you said, "Why me Lord? Why don't you pick on somebody else? They are not doing anything, why don't you send the problem on over to them? Why must I deal with it now?" When our lives turn upside down and inside out, we feel God is being unfair. When burdens press down upon us and become too heavy to bear, we say God is being unfair. When our bedroom turns into a sick room, God is being unfair. When it looks like God has not kept his promises in our lives, it looks like God is being unfair. When it appears as if the rascals and the scoundrels of the world have everything, but the righteous who are not supposed to be forsaken have nothing at all, we accuse God of being unfair.

Problems as Learning Opportunities

But if we would be honest about it, haven't we learned more from our problems than we have learned from our lives when the skies are blue and the sun is shining? If we were honest about it, we would recognize that we have learned more lessons when experiencing problems than during any other time in our lives. If we were honest about it, we would recognize that our problems have instructed and informed us better than any other vehicle. If we were honest, wouldn't we say that we have honed our coping strategies when we have had to deal with our problems? Often we respond to problems with dread and fear. But if we would just stand still for a moment and look at the problem as God's opportunity to strengthen our faith resources, fortify our belief systems, test our convictions, and prepare us for the struggles of tomorrow, we would fare much better. After all, how can you run with the horses if you can not even keep pace with the footmen?

It is interesting to me how we treat the problems that come along in our lives. Some of us develop amnesia. We forget we have a problem. We respond to difficulty by saying, "I have got a problem? No, I do not know about a problem. Do you know about a problem? Who me? Everything is fine." Some of us walk a problem. We walk a problem all over town, from one place to another. And if we do not have a problem to walk, then we walk somebody else's. We walk over here and we tell this one our problems, and then we walk over there to tell another one about our problems. We spend all week walking our problems all over town and then come to church on Sunday and tell our problems to the pastor. Some of us can not keep our mouths shut concerning things we ought to keep to ourselves. We talk our problems all over town. And if we do not have a problem to talk about, we discuss our neighbor's problems. We say, "Girl, did you hear? Have you found out? Oh, it's really bad and I don't know how they are going to make it. I don't think they are ever going to recover from that situation."

Some of us blame our problems on others. We say, "If I have a problem, it is your fault. You did it, you caused it, you arranged it, and if you were not in my life I would have no problems at all."

Scripture tells us about a woman with a problem. She lived outside of the geographical area in which Jesus conducted the majority of his ministry, along the borders of Tyre and Sidon, to the north of Jerusalem in an area that we know today as Lebanon. Jesus entered the house of a Gentile, which was uncharacteristic of a Jew because by doing so, his purity and ritual cleanliness were jeopardized. The woman approached Jesus and stated her circumstances. She had a daughter at home with an unclean spirit.

A Parent's Anguish

How many of you are parents, either by birth, adoption, or as spiritual parents? Isn't it amazing that when our children have a problem, when they hurt, when they are in a mess, when they are in a scrape, when they are in trouble, we also experience the same thing? You can be sixty-years-old, and your mother will hurt just as much as she did when you fell down and scraped your knee at five. Some time ago, there was a popular song whose lyrics said, "When something is wrong with my baby, something is wrong with me."[1] And there is an element of truth in that song. When something is wrong with our babies, something is also wrong with us. There are too many of our babies in the justice system and not enough of our babies in the educational system. Something is wrong. There are too many of our babies hanging around on the corner with nothing to do, and even if they had something to do, they would not want to do it. Something is wrong. There are too many of our babies employed by drug dealers. Something is wrong. There are too many of our babies living in the street, not because they have to but because they want to. Something is wrong. There are too many of our babies raising themselves and their friends because mama and daddy are too busy tripping the life fantastic. Something is wrong. There are too many of our babies dropping out and not enough standing up. Something is wrong. There are too many of our babies who are busy spending our money on what they want instead of coming to the church house for what they need. Something is wrong.

Stretching the Boundaries of Grace

The response of Jesus to the woman's plea can certainly be viewed as harsh, especially for one who had a reputation of compassion—one whom could solve the problems that the world deemed insolvable. But you must understand that this woman had a problem herself. She was not historically, culturally, or socially correct. Nor was she geographically located within the covenant of grace. She was part of the group that was on the outside looking in. So Jesus said to her, "I did not come for you. I did not come for your group. Your life does not stand up to those who are of the covenant for which I have come."[2]

This reflects the attitude that so many of us have in the righteous church houses across the land. We climb upon our pews and into our Bibles and we then turn around and look down upon our brothers and our sisters. We say to them, "You're not our kind," although they look like us. We look down our noses and say, "You don't dress like us. You don't smell like us. You don't live in my neighborhood. You don't work at my job, and what we have in here is not for you."

Jesus said to the woman, "I have come only for the lost sheep of Israel. The Gentile sheep like you are outside of my fold. I must first tend to the needs and to the feeding of Israel."[3] Jesus was imparting information to her to help her understand the parameters of his ministry. But the woman responded, "Even the dogs gather the crumbs from underneath the master's table."[4] Jesus marveled at her response and said, "You are a woman of great faith. Because you believe and because you answered in this way, I will do the very thing you've asked of me."[5]

Everyone is Included

By responding in that way, Jesus gave us a preview of both the cross and Calvary. By including this woman in his ministry at that point in time, we are reminded that the cross, his shed blood, and his empty tomb includes all of us. An exclusive ministry was broadened to include every chick and chittlering in the kingdom of God. No one can rightfully impose social, cultural, or geographical parameters on the grace of God. God included her and God has included you.

There may be some who want to exclude you, prevent you from obtaining what God has prepared for you, discriminate against you, or practice prejudice against you. But you do not have to worry about a thing because when they do it to you, they are doing it to God. God says, "Touch not my anointed and do my prophet no harm.["]6 So when people rise up with hatred and anger, just pray for them because God is going to deal with them. And I have lived long enough to know that you do not mess with God. So tell them, "God has already let me in and if you don't like it that's tough. If you have a bone to pick, you had better take it up with Jesus."

Recognize Jesus as Lord

So what can we learn from this woman and her problem that will help us with our problems? The gospels of Luke and John do not mention her, but the gospels of Mark and Matthew recognize and elevate her situation for our consideration. In the King James translation of the gospel of Mark, this woman refers to Jesus as Lord. This unnamed, incorrect woman is the only one in the gospel of Mark who recognizes Jesus as Lord. I invite you to search the Scriptures yourself. It was not any of the Pharisees, scribes, Sadducees, or a member of the Sanhedrin Court, his disciples, or the religious leaders of that day. It was this woman who recognized Jesus as Lord.

She reminds me of my grandparents who did not have much, just a pot behind the door and two pennies rubbed together. The only thing they knew was Jesus as Lord. They got down on their knees and prayed for their children, grandchildren, and their households. When the school system of this land would not educate us, they said "Jesus is Lord" and built schools all over the country. When the universities of this land said, "We will not train your young men and women as doctors and lawyers, they said, "That's alright, we will build our own universities and train our own lawyers, doctors, educators, psychologists, and philosophers. We will do it ourselves."

Now look at us. We possess more than our parents could ever hope or dream of. We are high on the hog and high on the pinnacle of material possession. But if you do not recognize Jesus as Lord, the very things with which God has blessed you will be lost.

Look at us. We can hardly keep hope alive. The institutions built by our foreparents on domestic wages, chauffeur wages, and babysitting wages exist today because their first priority was to recognize Jesus as Lord. So we, their heirs, who have so much more had better learn to recognize Jesus as Lord, also. Otherwise what we have will eventually go for naught.

Seek the Proper Counselor

The second thing we can learn from this woman is that she had enough sense to take her problem to Jesus. We walk and talk our problems all over town. Often, our girlfriends know more about our problems then the Lord does. We rehearse, nurse, analyze, and agonize over our problems. We go to the physician, the psychiatrist, the therapist, and every other type of professional in the land. And only when they say, "I can not help you," or "My textbook does not tell me how to treat your situation" do we consider going to Jesus. Only after the doctors have tried every procedure, every prescription, and every traditional and radical method of treatment and still nothing has helped, only then do we fall down on our knees and cry, "Father I stretch my hand to thee. No other help I know."[7] It is better to run to the Lord when trouble first appears at your door. When problems confront you, go to the Lord first, and let the Lord tell you where to go, whom to see, and when to see them.

Genuine Concern for Others

The third thing we can learn from this woman is that she went to Jesus on behalf of someone else. How much of our prayers are filled up with our own situation? It is true that sometimes we need to pray for ourselves, but we also need to take the time to pray on behalf of somebody else. We need to learn how to stand in the gap for somebody else. We need to learn how to help somebody else, how to lift somebody else, and how to go to bat for somebody else. Sometimes we must leave the comfort of our homes and go to the borders of Tyre and Sidon so that we can take somebody else's case to the Lord in prayer. If you do not, the same folk that you stepped over and looked down your nose at on your way up will be the ones you will meet on your way down.

Long Distance Blessings

The fourth thing we can see is that the result of her petition was granted through intercessory means. Jesus did not accompany the woman home or go into her house and lay his hands on her daughter. There was no holy oil, blessed coin, or prayer cloth that came through the mail. But when Jesus said it was done, it was done. He said to her, "When you get home the situation will already be rectified."[8]

That tells us that while we are praying for folk in one location, the Lord is working on it in another location. While you are at home praying for your co-worker, God is at your job fixing the situation. While you are at church praying about the home to which you are scared to return because you do not know what is going to meet you there, God is in your home working on it. One day those relatives who refuse to go to church with you will not know what hit them, because God is working on them right now. One day while driving down the street minding their own business or performing their chores, or waiting for their favorite television show to come on, God will smack them upside their heads. When you get home from church, they will say, "I think I'll go to church with you next Sunday." While they are watching television or reading the newspaper, God will break into their consciousness and will not let them go until they stand up and say "Yes Lord."

Handling Opposition

The final thing that is most impressive about this woman is the manner in which she handled opposition. We know she met opposition, for the gospel of Matthew tells us that the disciples of Jesus asked him to send her away. They said to Jesus, "She's bothering us, she's making a whole lot of noise, and we're sick of this. She isn't even our kind, so please send her away."[9] But when Jesus sets up a roadblock himself, observe how the sister responded. Did she cry or break down? Does she fall apart or lay down and wallow? Did she run home, pull her shades, take her phone off the hook and say, "Don't bother me about anything. I've had enough. I can't take any more today?" No. She did not do any of these things.

Instead of crying, she dug her heels in and said, "Wait a minute." She stood her ground and said, "I shall not be moved." There are some problems in our lives about which we must be as persistent as that woman. We must say, "I shall not be moved until I get an answer to my prayer. I am not moving until I see a change in my situation. I am going to pray, fast, and get in my Bible, but I am not moving so do not even bother to ask. I am going to stay right here until my change comes."

Isn't that what the neighbor did in the parable Jesus spoke in Luke 11:5-13? Although it was midnight, he kept knocking and knocking and knocking until someone got up to meet his need. In that parable Jesus said, "If this man would do this for his neighbor, what will your Father do who loves you? Would not he get up and meet your needs?" And what about that persistent woman in the judge's court who kept returning until the judge finally said, "Whatever this woman wants, please see to her need, and get her out of here."[10] If God loves you from everlasting to everlasting, won't God do the same thing for you?

That is what this sister did. She pressed until she got her blessing. What does that teach you and me? No matter how bad my problem or how perplexing the situation, I must press until I get my blessing. No matter how deep the valley or how hard the road is to climb, I must press until I get my blessing. I do not care how many mountains I have to jump over or how dark the night, I am going to press until I get my blessing. I do not care how many doors are slammed in my face with people telling me no, I am going to press until I get my blessing!

Meditation and Prayer

Lord, I have faith in you to guide me through the stormy areas of my life. Because your wisdom and power are infinite, that which frustrates and frightens me can be conquered as long as I trust you to lead the way. Therefore, I surrender each of my anxieties, large and small, to you. Teach me to listen for and obey your voice, so that I can respond to your leadership and guidance, allowing myself to take those steps that will usher in my own blessings.

Remove from me the temptation to wallow in self-pity induced by my problems. Replace it with a willingness to learn new lessons, see new opportunities, and take on a new perspective. And when circumstances stubbornly refuse to yield, give me the courage required to change myself, in spite of them.

Chapter Five:
The Workplace Blues

"When it comes to the cause of justice, I take no prisoners and I don't believe in compromising."

Mary Frances Berry

There are more statistics than necessary to prove that women are still global victims of a well entrenched system of patriarchal power which elevates one gender at the expense of the other. Pay scales are still unequal and glass ceilings remain intact. Indeed, patriarchal power and privilege rests at the foundation of most of our political, economic, cultural, and social institutions, thus making our world go round and round.

The woman in the following story was such a victim until one day the word of God was spoken into her life. At that moment, she was liberated from all forces that oppressed her, including the greedy men for whom she worked. So disturbed were the established powers by this unprecedented disruption of their exploitative yet routine business activity that they severely flogged and threw into jail the men of God who freed her.

So keep this story in mind the next time you experience inequity or insult in the workplace. Do not feel obliged to tolerate having those you have trained promoted over you or to acquiesce when your creative ideas are stolen and the credit for their success taken by others. You can defeat the workplace blues just as this slave girl did.

Women's Liberation: Jesus Style

Dr. J. Alfred Smith, Sr.

Scripture: Acts 16: 16-18

This Scripture introduces us to a nameless girl. Why is she nameless in this story? It is not because Luke has no respect for women. As the writer of both Luke and Acts, this great physician and author did more than any other writer in the New Testament to pay proper homage to women. Luke also was careful to describe the high place Jesus had for women in his life and ministry. Luke calls her a slave girl simply because she is the representative of untold and uncounted slave girls past and present who need liberation Jesus style. These enslaved and unempowered daughters of Eve are found in every country and are of every color, class, and caste. Her presence in our biblical narrative is a reminder to our consciences that these oppressed girls and young women cannot be ignored. You and I cannot enjoy the peace of a sweet night's rest when masses of girls and women are exploited for the pleasure, privilege, and power of patriarchy. Not even the selective promotion of a token woman to a position of puppet power can atone for prosperity gained at the high cost of making women's labor cheap. This double standard adversely affects scores of nameless, faceless women who work as nannies, maids, untenured professors, ministers on church staffs, and diplomats in government service. No matter where they work, a double standard is a double standard.

Luke states that this slave girl had a gift which earned a great deal of money for her owners. She was owned by greedy men. How many men owned her is unrevealed in the biblical narrative. But we do know that fathers in America never give their sons away to be married. They always give their daughters away. The marriage ceremony asks, "Who gives this woman to be married to this man?" The wife becomes the property of the man because she gives up her father's name to take on the name of her husband. Is the modern marriage ceremony an outdated ritual? Do men still own their wives? Do employers believe that they are to use women employees for company success? Do the working women have adequate child care, dental care, health care, and worker's compensation? Are they employed in dead-end jobs that afford no advancement? Are they provided with job training for upward mobility?

Not only do men capture and keep girls and women in moral, domestic, and vocational captivity, but sophisticated evil may engage women with middle management authority to oppress, exploit, or hold in captivity others of their own gender. A housewife can mistreat a nanny, a welfare worker can dehumanize a welfare client, a social worker can increase a client's feelings of inferiority, or a financial officer can refuse to counsel and guide a single parent into the green pastures of economic stability. A women's mission leader can turn her back on a young girl who gave birth to a baby out of wedlock. Sometimes this behavior of superiority and rejection is justified in the name of righteousness.

An Alternative to Slavery

But where sin abounded, grace much more abounds. Luke makes his point very clear. He explains to us that the nameless girl earned a great deal of money for her owners, but she followed Paul and the rest of us shouting, "These men are servants of the Most High God, who are telling you the way to be saved."

The nameless, faceless slave girl heard the message of salvation. She heard the message over and over again. She kept coming back for more good news. She returned again and again to hear the message of hope. She repeated for many days the good news of Paul's preaching and teaching. This nameless, faceless slave girl found an alternative and followed it. Persons in captivity will never discover liberation unless the church becomes the church and presents the gospel as the only viable alternative. Jesus Christ shut up in a book is not worth a passing look. Jesus imprisoned in a creed is a fruitless Lord indeed. But Jesus in the hearts of persons shows his tenderness again. What we are and what we have should make captives want to follow us. Captives should know that we are servants of the Most High God. Captives must understand that our mission is to tell people the way to salvation. Like Paul, we must be troubled when we see daughters, granddaughters and nieces in captivity. Like Paul, we must be so troubled until we turn around and work for liberation.

The story tells us that finally Paul became so troubled, he turned around and said to the evil spirit in the young woman, "In the name of Jesus Christ, I command you to come out of her." At that moment, the evil spirit left her. At that moment, which was the greatest moment of her life, she experienced women's liberation—Jesus style.

She was free. Evil men no longer owned her. She was free. Greedy men no longer enjoyed prosperity at her expense. She was free. Immoral men no longer obtained pleasure from her. She was free to be what God made her to be—free to love God and free to serve God. Never again would she have to depend upon exploitation by men for a livelihood. She was made free by Jesus who makes a way out of no way. Christ has a program of freedom for women of today.

I am glad about women's liberation—Jesus style. I am very glad about it because this same Jesus liberated my mother and my grandmother. Mother Amy and Grandmother Martha were poor, uneducated, working class women from the Mississippi Delta. However, Jesus gave them a liberation from the captivity of a racist past and the bondage of a segregated present. These wonderful women touched me and my brother, Joseph, with the liberating love of Jesus which enabled us to see ourselves as royal members of God's family, destined and designed to participate in God's kingdom building agenda. Now we rejoice and thank God for those two women who were liberated Jesus style. Because of their parenting, we can tell the world about that gracious God who entered the arena of our sinful captivity to set us free, to be all that God made us to be. Most of all, we are free to tell masculine peers that freedom in Christ for them also means full freedom in Christ for all sisters.

Let us be up and about God's mission of sharing the message of women's liberation, Jesus style.

Meditation and Prayer

God, life is unfair. Not because you are unfair, but because the world is filled with greedy, selfish, thoughtless people carrying their negative energy around in search of someone to dump it upon! Fortunately for us, we do not have to wage the war against such persons, events, or conditions alone, for we know that you are with us at all times.

Almighty God, we know that you can move mountains, part the sea, and force demons back into their pit. You can also squash racism, dispel sexism, and obliterate ageism on our behalf. But we must ask for your help or you will not butt into our affairs. So when confronted with the many injustices of this life, I will draw upon the power, wisdom and strength of the Divine, realizing that there is nothing that me and God, working as a team, can not handle.

Chapter Six:
My Sister, Myself

"If there is to be a sisterhood, not only must there be an examination of our history...but also how we deal with each other now."

Jennifer Henderson, activist

How we treat other women is often a reflection of how we see ourselves. If within the private recesses of our own minds and hearts, we are not convinced of our unique God-given beauty and worth, it is difficult to see the beauty and worth of others like us. So chances are that we will act out with cruel thoughts, words, or actions our lack of self-love upon another woman in whose eyes we see our own reflection.

The ideal of sisterhood encourages women to build trust among themselves and work together in seeking ways to solve problems that are unique to us. Very early in biblical history, however, the notion of sisterhood was kicked to the curb by a woman of social prominence who decided that the pursuit of her personal agenda was more important than her maid's most basic freedoms.

Unfortunately, some of us continue to kick the notion of sisterhood to the curb. But it does not have to be that way. We have a choice. The story that follows shows us how we should never, ever think of or treat another woman, if the ideal of sisterhood is to become real in our lives.

THAT WAS THEN...THIS IS NOW:
The story of Hagar and Sarai
Rev. Marsha Thomas

Scripture: Genesis 16:1-6

Throughout history we have seen evidence of God's hand in the lives of women: women of means and women of no means, white women and women of color, old women and young women, women of status in society and women of no status. Educated or uneducated, married or single, mothers or childless, God has had God's mighty hand on women throughout the generations.

Women have hurt others and we have felt our share of the pain. We have healed and we have helped others to heal. We have suffered and we have triumphed. We have come through many dangers, toils, and snares, and we have been able to shout hallelujah only by the grace of God.

Women have suffered greatly at the hands of some men. For centuries we have been property, entities for sale or barter, with no say about our own lives, hopes, dreams, or future. We all know that chattel has no rights, only the knowledge that you are at the beck and call of your master, always available to do his bidding.

Yes, women have suffered tremendously at the hands of some men. We have endured mistreatment of every variety: mental, emotional, and physical abuse, salary inequities in the workplace, reluctance or downright unholy resistance to women's participation in the priestly duties of the church, and frequent devaluing of a woman's role as a homemaker and nurturer of the children. Undeniably, all of this has been perpetuated by some men who were either uninformed, insecure, or unable to accept the fact that God's gifts are not gender specific. God's gifts are bestowed upon all persons and all levels of humankind. And yes, they are even bestowed upon women!

In some cases, however, women's treatment of other women has been far more hurtful, damaging, and devastating than anything we have endured at the hands of men. The story recorded in Genesis 16:1-6 is an example of this type of mistreatment. It tells a sordid tale of exploitation and persecution suffered by an Egyptian slave woman, Hagar, at the hands of her panicked, insecure Hebrew mistress, Sarai.

Hagar was a woman of color, handpicked by a wealthy herdsman named Abram during a trip to Egypt and presented to his wife Sarai as her handmaiden. Nothing is said about Hagar's family, so we do not really know much about her background. But let us imagine for a moment that because of her economic status, or lack thereof, her only means of livelihood was as a domestic. I imagine that she was an attractive, young woman, perhaps not yet 18, and in the prime of her life. Hagar was healthy, hardworking and vibrant, to the extent that she could be while working in someone else's house as a slave. She was the Hebrew woman's property, and as chattel she had no rights.

Hagar was expected to devote her life to fulfilling the desires of her mistress. If she had thoughts about what she wanted to do with her life, they did not matter because her sole mission was to please the woman for whom she worked. She belonged to someone else and therefore had few, if any options. That is just the way it was.

Now let me say a few words about Abram because I do not ever want to leave the men out of the picture. Abram was a herdsman. He was wealthy, socially prominent, successful, and probably retired. After all, he was 85-years-old. Although he had worked hard and acquired many worldly possessions, one very important thing was still missing from his life. Ten years before, God had made two promises to Abram. The first promise was that God would give Abram's descendants all the land extending from the River of Egypt to the Euphrates River, and the second promise was that God would give Abram a son borne of his own seed.

Abram believed and trusted God for the land. There was no problem with that. However, ten years had passed and there was still no sign of the promised son. At his age, Abram was starting to get a little nervous. He worried that perhaps his biological clock for making babies was running out. Abram had it all. He was healthy, wealthy, and wise, but he wanted more. He longed for a son—an heir to carry on the family name.

Now let us take a closer look at Sarai, the Hebrew mistress. The first verse in our Scripture tells us without a shadow of a doubt who Sarai was. She was "Abram's wife!" Isn't it interesting that first and foremost, this Hebrew woman is described not by her own gifts, talents, skills, size, shape, or appearance, but by her status as "Abram's wife." But that was pretty much the norm then. That is just the way it was. A woman's worth pivoted around her husband's status in the community. His reputation dictated her status and reputation. But even more important than monetary worth, education, involvement in the community, or artistic talents, a woman was honored by the number of male children she bore.

In those days, a woman's fertility was revered. It increased her worth and affirmed her usefulness to her husband and her community. The pressure to "produce" must have been tremendous, and I imagine that Sarai wanted very much to fulfill her expected role and bear Abram a son. However, she had a serious problem. The Scripture tells us that Sarai had no children and was 76 years old, long past her childbearing years. Never mind that Sarai had social standing, she was barren. Forget about all of her husband's material wealth, she was barren. No matter that she was beautiful, she was still barren. She was less than a woman in the eyes of the Hebrew community. And although Abram loved her, I am sure she felt his disappointment that she had not given him the son that God had promised. It is very sad that many women blame themselves for things that are totally out of their control. But that's another story!

Sarai's Bondage—Hagar's Awakening

One of the important lessons of this story is how Sarai felt about herself. Hagar may have been a slave, but Sarai was definitely in bondage! As she watched the years come and go during which God's prophetic promise remained unfulfilled, Sarai became a desperate, depressed, childless woman who would apparently stop at nothing to satisfy her community's criteria for womanhood. She demonstrated that she would go to any length to make herself feel whole and complete as a woman and to make her husband proud. She would even go as far as taking matters into her own hands to fulfill a promise that God had made but had not yet brought to completion. God was moving much too slowly for Sarai, so she came up with her own plan to fix the situation.

Sarai was completely frustrated—frustrated enough to ask her husband to participate in an ill-fated plan designed to elevate her own self-esteem, make her husband proud, and bring about the fulfillment of God's long overdue promise. But in doing so, she misused another woman—a slave woman who believed she had no power or authority, not even over her own life.

Because she could see no other way, the barren Hebrew

85

woman put Hagar in a very tough situation. She announced to Hagar that she was to sleep with Abram. What on earth was Hagar to do? Say no to her mistress, employer, and owner? I don't think so. In exchange for the security of a roof over her head and food in her mouth, Hagar complied with Sarai's directive.

And so it was. Hagar slept with Abram, a co-conspirator in this no-win plan, and she became pregnant. Sarai thought she had it made and was surely on her way to high position and status in the community. She envisioned Abram as the proud father, smiling and happy, passing out cigars to all his homeboy herdsmen. And she assumed Hagar would continue to behave as a good little slave girl by having the baby, keeping quiet, and going on with her life. Business would continue as usual for everyone.

But after she discovered she was pregnant, something came over Hagar. She began to despise what Sarai had done. You know, it may take a while, but sometimes we have to get mad before we can get glad. Sometimes anger can provide the momentum to get us out of a rut and move us in new directions. Hagar began to resent how Sarai mistreated her, manipulated her, and tried to control her life. Suddenly, things were not so good anymore. Even a palace and a good steak were not enough to keep this little Black girl a slave. Hagar had tolerated the mistress-slave arrangement for too long, and now something told her to break free and run. The Scriptures tell us that Hagar really did not know where she was going—she just knew she wanted to get out of Sarai's house.

The Good News

This story took place over 2,000 years ago. Since that was then and this is now, you are probably wondering, "What's the point? What does this story have to do with me?"

The first piece of good news is that no matter how hopeless things appear, God is in control. Secondly, we must remember that when God makes a promise, it is God's job to keep it, and our job to believe it and then wait on God to fulfill it. When we panic, like Sarai, and take matters into our own hands, we generally make a real mess of things!

We can also learn a great deal about sisterhood from Hagar and Sarai. We can learn that we do not have to envy other women because of what or who they have, because God has a plan for every one of us—a plan that sometimes defies time, circumstances, and all that our finite minds can understand. Somewhere in our past, we may have heard, thought, or said something malicious about another sister— statements such as, "She thinks she's so much because she's got that good job and she's making all of that money. You know how she got that job, don't you?"

Well that was then, but this is now. The good news of the Gospel says that we can do all things through Christ Jesus who strengthens us—but in God's good time! We do not have to put another woman down so that we can be lifted up.

If Sarai had just trusted God and been a little more patient, she would have experienced the glory of God's fulfilled promise, just as we can today! Instead, for her own selfish benefit, she allowed her economic and cultural status to put dangerous distance between herself and her maid, thereby weakening the fabric of global sisterhood. As a result, their relationship moved further and further away from what God intends for all of his daughters—a kinship that affirms the worth of all women and transcends worldy titles and descriptions.

Times have changed. That was then and this is now. Fortunately, we are no longer identified exclusively by who we are married to or revered simply for having male children. Sisters of all colors, races, ages, and economic circumstances are beginning to realize that we have choices, the choices that God gives us as we strive to be all that God wants us to be. We do not have to remain in the bondage of low self-esteem, be a slave to keeping up with Ms. Jones, or remain shackled by the "I can't live my life without a man" mentality! That was then but this is now. Now is a perfect time for us to celebrate our sisterhood and proclaim our newly found freedom in the Lord. We can read the story of Sarai and Hagar and say, "That was then, but this is now."

Sisters, we have the opportunity today to treat other women with the dignity and respect that God intended for all of us, no matter where we live or what we do for a living. Ironically, as the story unfolds, we see that Hagar was not the one in the deepest bondage. Without a doubt, Hagar was a slave, but Sarai was imprisoned by the yardstick of her own community, which gave her a clear message that she did not measure up as a woman unless she bore a son. We must remember that God is more powerful than societal expectations and our sometimes distorted view of who or what we think we should be. The God we serve is able to liberate us from dangerous thinking and destructive behavior that can push us to the edge like Sarai.

God can liberate us from the need to make demeaning comments about other women and God can even deliver us from making demeaning comments about ourselves—the "I'm too fat, too dark, too light, not smart enough" rhetoric. And God is truly able to deliver us from competition for a man! If we just trust God, we can be delivered from all that Sarai was struggling with—all of those forces within us that may compel us to mistreat our sisters as Sarai did. And we can certainly be delivered from the low self-esteem that must have plagued the Egyptian handmaiden.

Hagar was a victim of circumstance—she had no money, no education, and no skills. On the other hand, Sarai was a "legend in her own mind," which allowed her to pathetically abuse her own power. But that was then and this is now! I am believing that this is a new day for women. God is doing something new with us. Let us learn from Sarai and Hagar, and rejoice together as we allow God to move in bold new ways in our lives. Imagine how sisterhood could be strengthened if, instead of envying another woman, you complimented her. Or suppose you congratulated another sister on her promotion, although you were passed over. Or if you were happy for your girlfriends with companions, even if you are still searching for your soulmate.

We might find it easier to affirm another woman, regardless of race, culture, or economic circumstance, if we know who we are and whose we are. We are daughters of the King and we lack nothing! We are complete in Christ Jesus and have access to God's abundant world. The moment we truly believe this is the moment we will be set free. God can change our motives from power, control, manipulation, and competition to a spirit of cooperation, support, encouragement, and love. Let us receive the fulfillment of God's promise right now!

Meditation and Prayer

Lord, help me understand that by acknowledging and encouraging the beauty and talent within others, I will discover the beauty and talent within me. I confess any hurtful acts or statements I have committed against others—especially my sister-girlfriends. Please forgive me and help us to forgive each other. Help us to build sturdy friendships through which we can realize your highest calling in our lives.

Chapter Seven:
It's Time to Make a Change

"I thought I could change the world. It took me one hundred years to figure out that I can't change the world. I can only change Bessie. And honey, that ain't easy, either."

Bessie Delany

What is your divine purpose? Why were you placed on this earth? Who or what are you trying to become? Are you actively working toward your vision of your highest and greatest self, or are you stuck in a rut of mundane, everyday sameness? If you are stuck, what is your blueprint for escape? Do you have a plan or are you waiting to be rescued from your personal, private mess by Prince Charming, the lottery, or some other equally mysterious phenomenon?

The only way we can change our lives is by making a firm decision to do so and then following through with positive action. We learned that from Terry McMillan's blockbuster novel, **Waiting to Exhale.** *While most of the controversy generated by that novel centered around the blustery male-female relationships it depicted, there was much more to Ms. McMillan's story than that. The "Waiting to Exhale" syndrome can plague anyone, but when it does, God has given us a plan for breaking free. That plan is revealed in the following story.*

Breaking Free from the Waiting to Exhale Syndrome

Dr. Jeanne L. Porter

Scripture: John 5:1-15

I want to talk about breaking free from the "Waiting to Exhale" syndrome. Perhaps you have never heard of the *"Waiting to Exhale"* syndrome. Although there has been a lot of discussion surrounding Terry McMillan's third novel,[1] I do not want to talk about the novel itself. Instead, I want to teach you how to be free from the syndrome that is portrayed by the characters in the story.

Let us start by defining what a syndrome is. A syndrome is a pattern of behavior that is chronic, recurring, and usually unhealthy. It is defined as a group of signs and symptoms that occur together and characterize a particular abnormality.[2] The Waiting to Exhale syndrome is not normal, it is not natural, and it is definitely not what the Lord intends for his followers.

The Waiting to Exhale syndrome is not something that scientists have identified, so you can not go to the Center for Disease Control or the National Institutes of Health to learn more about it or to get a cure for it. *Waiting to Exhale* became popular in the early 1990's when Terry McMillan published her blockbuster novel by that name in which the lives of four African American women were chronicled. Time and time again, these women found themselves in relationships that were unhealthy. Yet, each of them kept holding their breath, thinking that the next man they met would be their "knight in shining armor." But because they were locked into certain behavior patterns, the women continued to meet the same type of men. They ignored the signs that their own behavior was much of the source of their dilemmas, yet kept hoping that each new man they met would be different than the ones from the past.

When the book was made into a movie, a lot of its viewers criticized McMillan and accused her of male bashing. Others agreed that her portrayal of black, single women was accurate but began to perpetuate stereotypes. During the midst of the controversy, I began to see beyond the movie to the reality undergirding the syndrome that McMillan was attempting to illustrate. When looking beyond the symptoms and seeing the malady itself, it becomes apparent that this syndrome does not impact only young, black, single women. It impacts men, women, African American, European American, Hispanic, Asian, old, young, employed, and over-employed, if there be such a thing. It is really about a state of mind, a view of life, and a pattern of behavior that people hold on to that keeps them stuck and unable to progress.

We see a lot of people, even in the body of Christ, who are frustrated, stuck, and wondering, "What's wrong with my life?" When you remain in unhealthy situations long after becoming aware of their negative impact upon your health, then honey, you are waiting to exhale! You are holding your breath, waiting and hoping that something else or someone else can bring fulfillment to your life. You are ignoring the signs around you that your current situation is not where you belong or where you are supposed to be, or you are too weak or too dependent upon crutches to get out of your mess. Has anyone ever been there?

Recognizing the Symptoms

Here are some other ways to recognize the Waiting to Exhale syndrome. You may see it in someone that you know. Some folk's finances are in a mess because the spending pattern they continue to employ gets them in trouble time and time again. Instead of trying to take proactive steps to get out of debt, they are waiting to hit the lottery. Now I know that some of you come from the old school and you are saying, "I do not play the lottery." Well, there are a number of you who are waiting for the prize patrol. You are waiting for Ed McMahon to come by and announce that you have won the sweepstakes!

Or what about those people who hold a job for which they are overqualified or frustrated with because they have been there twenty years and are not getting anywhere? But, instead of utilizing the gifts that God has given them to explore new opportunities, they sit where they are, waiting for the boss to move on, so they can take his or her place.

Then there are husbands and wives who are waiting for the kids to move out. "When the kids are gone, we can really live," they say! And there are those who are waiting to retire. It all reflects the same malady and the same issues.

I think that as believers in Christ, God wants us to be very clear concerning our purpose. He does not want us to lead lives of frustration and stagnation. He is saying, "I have so much for you and so many places to take you in me that you don't have to sit there and be frustrated!"

So as you see, the underlying commonality of these people is that they are waiting, holding their breaths and saying, "I can't live right now." It reminds me of when we were children waiting for some type of secret Santa or magical event to happen. We would hold our breaths, close our eyes, cross our fingers and say, "I know this is the one for me." Has anyone ever been there?

In the spiritual realm, God is saying to us that the same thing is happening too many times right now. And he wants us to let go, take a deep breath, uncross our fingers and know that we can live according to his Word and reap all of the precious promises that he has given to us. He wants us to know that he desires to take us from frustration to liberty. He desires to take us from bondage to the promised land!

Pool Side Events - A Closer Examination

Let us examine our biblical text, John 5:1-15, more closely to look at a man who was waiting to exhale. This passage tells us of a situation that occurred during one of the feasts of the Jews. It was a time of celebration, and the site was Jerusalem, the center of religious activity. Jerusalem was an ancient city and by the time of Christ, it had become the center of worship for the Jews. It was a walled city, and within those walls were eight gates and thirty-four towers.

There was one particular gate known as the sheep gate. It was situated in the north course of Jerusalem, within the walls themselves. In the olden days, the worshipers would pass through the sheep gate with their sheep on their way to the temple. They would wash their sheep by dipping them into the pool, so that they could offer God a clean sacrifice. The pool was called Bethesda, which in the Aramaic language meant "outpouring of God's grace." I call it "the place of grace."

When Jesus came to the town on this particular occasion, he saw that sheep were no longer being brought into the gate and washed in the pool. Instead he saw human beings who had journeyed to this region in search of some help lying on the porches outside of the pool. They were sick folk. Impotent folk. Powerless folk. There they were, lined up on the porches. Instead of jumping into the pool at this place of grace and enjoying the blessings that accompany an outpouring of grace, they were lying on the pool's outskirts, in a state of malaise.

Are You On the Porch or In the Pool?

Has anyone ever come to church and seen the saints of God moving around and rejoicing, but instead of joining in, you remained on the outskirts? Does anyone ever wonder why folks do not come on inside the house of God where God is moving and delivering in our midst? Too many folks stay outside on the porches, rocking in their rocking chairs while God is saying, "Come on in the pool where I am moving. I can fill you with my Spirit and I can give you a special dose of anointing, a touch that will keep you strong and powerful." Someone knows what I mean. You used to be out on the porches but you now can say, "God told me to come on into the pool!"

So here we have five porches around the sheep gate that were filled with great multitudes of sick people. These multitudes include those who were blind, lame, and paralyzed. What God began to show me is that we have the same thing happening right now. Today, however, it is not those with physical disabilities that I am talking about, but those with spiritual disabilities. We have a bunch of spiritually sick folk on the outside who need to come inside.

Think about situations you have been in. I have been in situations in which the people around me were blind—they had no vision concerning what God was doing. And as God began to move me out, he told me, "If you're going to have my vision, you've got to do what I say, because the people around you can't see what I'm doing. They won't understand it and they'll think you are crazy!" The same thing will happen to you as you begin to seriously study the word of God and develop a prayer life. Folks will say, "Oh, it doesn't take all of that." That is when you will know that they are not where you are. They are still out on the porch, but you are moving in!

Jesus also saw on those porches some lame folks. Again, I am not talking about folks in wheelchairs or with crutches. I am talking about folks without any physical limitations who could not walk straight if you paid them. God says, "Walk in the straight path by doing as I say."[3] But because they're rebellious, stiff-necked, and hard-hearted, they do things their own way. They remind me of Frank Sinatra's song, "I Did It My Way." When God starts moving and says to you, "I want to take you over there," you can not stay with those lame folks and you can not keep those lame excuses. You have got to walk where God wants you to walk, and you have got to do it God's way.

Who else was there? There were some people who were paralyzed. Again, I am not talking about quadriplegics. I am talking about folks who are not going anywhere and are doing nothing with their lives. We are talking about spiritually stuck folks who do not know how to lead and who do not know how to follow. They just get in the way.

I hear God saying that if we are going to build his kingdom here on earth, we need some leaders. We need some agents down here who do not mind getting on their knees to pray Satan's kingdom down. They do not mind binding something up or loosing something in the name of Jesus. God says, "If we are going to win this world, people are going to have to know that you are different because you have a new faith, you are a new creation, you have a new spirit, and you have a new attitude!"

Buying into a Myth

So in our text we see many people with one thing in common—they were waiting for the mysterious moving of the waters. But why were they waiting for this event to occur?

Popular tradition of that day held that this particular pool was often visited by an angel who came down to trouble the water and heal the first one who stepped in of whatever disease he had. However, there is no evidence throughout the rest of the Scripture that this ever really happened. Therefore, I believe John, the text's writer, is merely recounting a popular myth of his times, while also telling us that this myth explains the size of the crowds and why they were waiting.[4]

With that in mind, it is easy to understand the mind set of those lingering at the outskirts of the pool because we have during present times popular myths upon which many people have become dependent. And instead of going to Jesus, we witness our contemporaries relying upon these popular myths to solve their problems.

For instance, how many people do you know who dial

1-900-Psychic? Jesus said, "I'll give you a clear path to get you to what you need in me,"[5] but instead we see people asking a psychic to reveal their future. Meanwhile, Jesus is telling us he has got everything we need. You do not need to call the Psychic Network because Jesus said, "I have left my testament right here for you. Whatever you need, I have it for you."[6]

Compete with Others or Cooperate with the Spirit?

I get tickled when I think that if I had been there at that pool side, and they told me that this healing spring was going to bubble up every so often, I probably would have been on the edge of the pool. As soon as it looked like it was about to bubble up, I would have jumped right in. A friend of mine said that she would have lived in the pool and you could not have gotten her out of it, if that was where she was going to get her healing.

Then God encouraged me to think about it some more and he began to show me some things. The popular myth said that when the water bubbled up, only the first one into the pool could be healed, although there were many folks present who needed healing. The very system that had been devised by popular culture implied that the way to healing was divisive and competitive. And so what I see is the potential for people to knock over one another and push others out of the way to get to the front of the line when the pool began

103

to bubble.

But God does not work like that, does he? When Jesus pours out his blessings, it is not about competing with one another. There is enough of what the Lord has to go around for everybody. If God has a blessing for you, nobody can take it away from you! And because God blesses you does not mean that he can not bless me at the same time. He said, "I will pour out of my Spirit upon all flesh,"[7] not just a selected few. Not just one or two, not just the ones who get to the pool first, but on all flesh! That is how God works. God desires that we all be blessed!

Acknowledging Our Need to Exhale

I am sure that when Jesus looked into that crowd, it saddened him to realize that people were stuck where they were, and that they attributed their helplessness to "waiting on the Lord" instead of "waiting to exhale." So Jesus picks out one helpless man from the crowd to illustrate his ability to change a person's life.

I can see Jesus looking at this man, realizing that he had been there for a very long time. Verse six of our text, in one of the translations from its Greek origins, says "Jesus noticed him." That spoke to me mightily because it tells me that God is concerned about the individual. Thousands of folks were there, yet Jesus saw that one person. Something happens when God notices you, because at that moment, he begins to lock into your situation and says to you, "I know what you need and I'm ready and able to fulfill it." God cares about the needs of each individual.

The first thing we must understand is that there are circumstances in our lives that keep us trapped, and we need to rid ourselves of them. The apostle Paul referred to this as "laying aside every weight and sin that does so easily beset us."[8] As individuals, we have to acknowledge when and if we are waiting to exhale. Too often, we want to fake it by coming to church wearing false faces, as if everything were all right. But God is saying that if you are really waiting to exhale, you need to acknowledge it. I have acknowledged the times when I was waiting to exhale. I acknowledged when I was looking for Mr. Prince Charming, and God said to me, "I'm all the Prince Charming you are going to get at this present time!"

And some of you brothers have been in the same place. You are looking for Ms. Right but God is saying that right now, he wants you in his Word and on your knees. He is saying, "I want you to develop a relationship with me so that when I send the right one your way, you'll be in position to receive her and be the man that I'm calling for you to be."

Because this man had been by the pool for such a long time, I am sure he had begun to accept his plight and his lot in life. In the same way, each of us at some point in our lives must look around and say, "I am waiting to exhale. Something is not working and I'm looking for a way to fix it." You have got to examine your home life, community life, job life, relationships, and so on, and then ask, "What is wrong with this picture?" You must recognize that you are not created to just lie there. God desires that you move because "in him we live and move and have our being."[9] That there is a point in life that you have got to acknowledge that there has got to be more to life than frustration and stagnation. The man by the pool had to acknowledge that.

Next, God shows us through this text the seven steps to breaking free from our "waiting to exhale" syndromes.

Step One: Desiring Wholeness

The first step to freedom is to make up in your mind that you want to be whole. In verse six of our text, Jesus looked at the man, knowing he had been there for a very long time, and asked him, "Do you want to be made well? Do you want to be made whole?"

Sometimes when God asks that question, many people do not know how to answer it. We do not know what it would take to make us whole or well. In case you are unsure, let me just remind you what you should want and need from God. God wants you to have the abundant life. God desires that you prosper in your soul and your body. God desires that your whole spirit, soul, and body be sanctified and kept blameless. God desires that you be more than a conqueror, not somebody who is beat up on all the time. God has plans and desires for you that are good, and that will give you a future and a hope.[10]

I had to get to the point in my life where I wanted everything that God had for me. I had to become clear on God's destiny and purpose for me and then decide if that was what I wanted, too. Once I got that down in my spirit, I was able to have some real joy, the kind that an antidepressant is unable to provide. I was able to get happy in Jesus and enjoy a blessedness that no one could take away. And when others tried to mess with me, I knew that God was on my side. "And if God is for us, then who can be against us?"[11] Up to that point, I was frustrated, moody, and always wondering why I could not get this or that. God said, "Don't worry about it. The steps of a righteous person are ordered by the Lord. You just relax, take a deep breath, and let me handle it."[12] Sit back and leave the driving to God!

Now some people do not want to be whole. Some people do not want to be well because it is easier for them to stay in their mess. After all, once you become identified as a sick person, you get lots of pity. Sometimes people feel that it is easier to stay in their mess and continue receiving pity than it is to move. But God is saying, "To change this world, I need whole people." Who wants to be whole? I want you to come to grips with that.

Step Two: Stop Making Excuses

When Jesus asked, "Do you want to be made whole?," the man's response was, "Sir, I do not have anyone to put me in the pool." That was an excuse. And Jesus is saying to us today, "I want you to be whole, but I do not want any more excuses." We have a tendency to make excuses, but if God desires for you to have something, he will make a way, in spite of the obstacles.

I heard someone say, "This is a racist society and a sexist society, so I can not do this or that." But God is asking, "Do you want to be made whole? If so, leave the "isms" up to me." I hear others saying, "But I came from the wrong side of the tracks," or "My mother didn't love me," or "I didn't know who my father was." But God is saying, "I didn't ask you that. I want to know if you want to be made whole?" But I am not tall enough! I am not short enough! And God still responds, "But do you want to be made whole?" If so, everything else is irrelevant because with God, all things are possible. He can break down every single barrier and move anything blocking your way.[13] You just need to make up in your mind that you want to be whole, quit making excuses and God says, "I will help you to break free."

Too many of us believe that somebody else owes us something and we need to be rescued. Fundamentally, that is what the man in our text is saying—"There's nobody here to rescue me." God said to him, "Look, you are waiting for the angel but who do you think dispatches the angels? I am here in your midst right now and I am ready to give you the healing that you've been waiting for! Brother, do you really want to be made whole? Or are you lying here because you have gotten accustomed to this position, you are stuck, and you really do not want to get up?"

Once you can stop making excuses, a change is required in the way you see things.[14] What happens when we get stuck is we find ourselves repeating habits and modes of behavior that reflect our thinking patterns. We get comfortable in the position in which we are stuck. We get accustomed to seeing folks who are not moving just like us and we begin to think that is natural.

And so literally, it takes a shift from your way to God's way. In your way, you will keep laying around with folks who are stuck themselves, but in God's way, you will get up and you will walk in faith. In your way, you will depend on an uncertain future, but in God's way, you will hope in the certainty of Jesus Christ. In your way, you will fight and compete to be first, but in God's way, you will cooperate with the Spirit and do what the Spirit is leading you to do. In your way, you will wait on somebody to help you, but in God's way, you will help yourself through the power of the Holy Spirit. In your way, you will complain when others do not help you the way you think they should. But in God's way, you will get up and help somebody else. In your way, you will make excuses for why you are not well, but in God's way, he will take away all of the excuses, because he has nailed them to the cross.

Step Three: Rise!

After you stop making excuses, the moment of truth will

come. That is when it is time to rise.

Look at verse seven again real closely. When confronted and challenged by Jesus, the man begins to tell on himself. He says, "While I am coming, another steps down before me." We thought this man could not move, scoot, crawl or do anything else. But he tells on himself when he says, "When I am coming." He reveals that he can move at least a little bit. He exposed his potential!

God knows what you are capable of doing. He is already aware of your potential, but is waiting for you to discover it within yourself. And once you realize the little you can do, with the Lord's help, you can do so much more. The Lord motivates us and prods us to action through his words and promptings within our human spirit. He says, "Get up from there! No more laying down. No more sitting there." This is your hour! This is your day in which you can be made whole! Rise! His very word resurrects life into our spirits and inspires us to action. His words are spirit and life.[15]

Step Four: Pick up your bed!

Why did Jesus give the man in our text the command, "Pick up your bed?" Because he knew that the pallet by the side of the pool had become the man's virtual home. He had gotten comfortable there. All of his possessions were there and his identity had become entwined in that place. I hear Jesus saying, "Get all that stuff up. Fold it up and let's get it out of here. Because if you leave it there, you will be tempted to come back to it."

In other words, when it is time to break with the past, it is best to break completely because if you leave some vestiges behind, you will be too tempted to return. For many people who are waiting to exhale, it is time to take up your bed, take ownership of your stuff, and understand the consequences of your actions. It is time to grow up in Jesus Christ.

Step Five: Walk!

Now remember we have in our text a man who could not move, yet Jesus says to him, "Walk!" Why? Because when the word of God is infused into your life, you can do things that you never thought you could do before. God is saying to us right now, "Walk in faith and walk by faith."[16] You may not know how you are going to make the second step, but he said that the first step is the biggest one. So take it. Just launch out there, like Abraham did,[17] and God will take care of you every step of the way. How many want to walk in faith today? How many want to go to the next level in God? How many want to be the men and women that God is calling for? He said, "You must walk in faith. Even if you begin with baby steps, you must walk. Other individuals can not carry you, but I can."

Step Six: Be Prepared for Adversities

When you decide that you are going to go to the next level in God and be free of past bondage, you are going to be confronted by some adversity because the devil does not want to see any of us free. For instance, when you make up in your mind that you are going to fast and pray, that is when your job decides to have a free luncheon. You receive more invitations than ever to go out to lunch with co-workers on the day you decide to fast in order to get in touch with God. The moment you decide that you are going to come out to midweek Bible study is when you learn you have got to work late. Or it is the moment when everything seems to break loose and go crazy. The adversary does not want to see you prosper. He knows that the secret to our success is to develop a close relationship with Jesus. The moment that you decide to pray before going to bed is the night you are going to fall asleep on the floor!

And the moment you decide to become integrated into the church family is when your friends from the world will start talking about you even more. They may say things like, "Oh, you think you're all that? Ms. or Mr. Holiness, huh?" But if that is what it takes, then you have got to say goodbye to those friends because God is telling you to take up your bed and walk. You must be ready for the confrontation.

In verses nine through twelve of our text, we see that after the man began to walk, he was confronted by a group of religious leaders who asked him, "What are you doing being cured on the Sabbath day?"[18] Now what kind of question is that? They should have been rejoicing that the man was cured! When you become whole and start thinking right, talking right, walking right, and living right, someone is going to ask you, "What do you think you are doing?" But how many know that it does not matter what anybody else says? If your spirit desires to know God and to get more from God, it really does not matter. But be ready for the confrontation. Do not let it throw you off guard, confuse you, or make you want to go back. Be prepared for adversity and resist it!

Step Seven: Give God the Glory

In verse fifteen of our text, the man tells those who confronted him that it was Jesus who healed him. He testifies to the healing power of Jesus Christ. If others confront you as you are moving into the new realm that God has for you, do not get defensive and try to explain things away. Just testify to what God is doing in your life. If God is doing something good for you, just tell it and witness to the power of Jesus Christ! It is going to take changed lives to change this world. As your life is being changed, testify and talk about it. Your sustained freedom is tied to your faithful confession. Your freedom is based upon the wonderful work and power of God. The Lord has found you and has spoken deliverance and life into your very existence.

Finally, giving God glory through praise and worship are key elements in the process of breaking free from the Waiting to Exhale syndrome. Worship ushers you into God's presence, and his presence provides everything you need to walk in victory. Like the delivered man in our text, you will come to recognize Jesus and acknowledge his move in your life.

So you do not have to wait to exhale. You can take a deep breath and flow in the move of God. You can let go of patterns that blocked you and hindered you. You can be free!

Meditation and Prayer

Lord, help me to take an honest, unadulterated look at myself and my life. Point out to me the places in my life where I have fallen victim to the *Waiting to Exhale* syndrome. If I am causing some of my problems myself, standing in my own way, or blocking my own progress, help me to break free. Please do not allow me to sabotage my own quest to become whole.

Lord, remind me that in any situation, I have the power to determine the flow of consequences toward me. Old habits and entrenched behaviors may knock at my door, but I do not have to let them in! I am free to choose a new way, and in doing so, open the door to a new experience.

Chapter Eight:
Taming a Wild Woman

"When we remember we are all mad, the mysteries disappear and life stands explained."

Mark Twain

Surely you know at least one wild woman. Totally out of control, she feeds on a steady diet of self-destructive activity. She can not seem to decipher between what is good for her and what is not. She is her own worse enemy, seemingly incapable of imposing any limitations on her self-inflicted pain.

She is not necessarily violent. Usually the only victim of her self-deprecating behavior is herself. She justifies her self-destructive lifestyle with a distorted understanding of liberation. So when confronted by others with the irrationality of her acts, she is quick to tell you that because she is grown, she can do as she pleases. She thinks she is totally free, living above the hypocritical and encumbering interference of others. But we know the truth about this woman—she is teetering on the brink of madness.

Is there any hope for her? Of course there is. Find out how a wild woman (or man) can experience a reversal of fortune.

Jesus Made The Difference

Dr. Jeremiah A. Wright, Jr.

Scripture: Luke 8:1-3; II Corinthians 5:17

The New Revised Standard version of the Bible translates Second Corinthians 5:17 this way: "If anyone is in Christ, there is a new creation. Everything old has passed away. Everything has become new." Paul's words, in his second letter to the church in Corinth were a testimony of how his own life had been touched personally by the hand of Jesus. Paul's words also summarize in many ways the testimony of another life that we catch a glimpse of in the eighth chapter of the gospel of Luke—Mary of Magdala.

Mary was one of the women disciples. Mary went where Jesus went—through the cities, through the villages, through the towns, and all throughout Galilee. Mary was there when the Lord preached and Mary was there when the Lord talked. She heard him speak many of the parables we read in the Scriptures. She heard them from the lips of the one who said "I am." You and I read the word of God, but think about this—Mary was there to hear the word. She heard the Word who was in the beginning with God and who was God. She heard the Word by whom all things were made and without whom was not anything made that was made. She heard the Word that became flesh and dwelt among us. Mary was in the "we" that the gospel writer is referring to when he says, "We beheld his glory, the glory as of the Father's only Son, full of grace and truth."[1]

Mary was there when Jesus healed that man who lived in a cemetery, the one whom the people came out to see for themselves and found clothed in his right mind. Mary was there in the eighth chapter of Luke when Jesus entered the precincts and Jairus ran up to him, fell at his feet, and begged him to come and put his hands on his twelve-year-old daughter who was dying. Mary was there when the woman with the issue of blood pressed her way through the crowd saying, "If I can just touch the hem of his garment, I know that I can be made well."[2] Mary was there when Jesus said to her, "Daughter, your faith has made you well. Go in peace."[3] You and I can only read or hear about it. But Mary was right there and saw it all with her own eyes.

In the next chapter, Mary was right there—out in the desert, near the town of Bethsaida, a lonely place—when the Lord fed five thousand men, not including the women and children.[4] Mary was one of the women who was not counted, but she was fed anyhow. She was fed on the bread of heaven by the Bread of Heaven with five loaves of bread and two fish. She saw Jesus give thanks, lift the five loaves and two fishes up to heaven, bless them, and break them. She saw him do what no other man could do. She saw the brothers take up twelve baskets of leftovers—leftovers after feeding over ten thousand—leftovers from five loaves and two fish. Mary did not need anybody to tell her anything about Jesus and his miracles! She was there to see it for herself!

Eight days later in this same chapter, Mary was there when Peter, James, and John went up a mountain with Jesus. She was there when a daddy brought his son to the disciples to be cured and they could not cure him. Mary was one of the women disciples, and according to Luke, she was one of the women who provided for the Lord and his ministry out of her resources. She gave her money to the Lord. She met the need whenever there was one. She was not like we are, stingy and stupid, trying to stash her cash. When the Lord needed money, she gave what she had and she gave what she could. Mary was a woman who loved the Lord. No wonder she was the last one at the cross and the first one at the tomb! Jesus had made a difference in her life!

How do we know that Jesus had made a difference in Mary's life? If we go back and look at verse two of the eighth chapter of Luke, it tells us that before Jesus, Mary had been a pistol. She did not have just one evil spirit. She did not have just one disease. Mary had seven demons living on the inside of her. Seven.

Wrestling With Demons: The Demon of Lust

Like Mary, each of us wrestles with demons. In fact, some of us right now are wrestling with the demon of lust.

We know what we are supposed to do, but we somehow just can not seem to find the strength to do it. That demon has got us and he has got us good. And we will try all kinds of intellectual games to dress this demon up in the garments of respectability. We justify our actions by saying things like: "How do you know it is wrong? After all, there are different mores for various cultures. Why in Africa right now there are some cultures where polygamy is legal. If you look back in the Bible days, Abraham had Sarah and Hagar. Jacob had Leah and Rachel plus Zilpah and Bilhah. So how does monogamy get to be the norm or the practice that is superior to other practices?" We play all kinds of intellectual games!

One sister told me her husband was into ancient Egyptian religion. Then she clarified her statement by saying he was her ex-husband. She said being involved in that religion was a monstrous and elaborate rationalization for him and his partners to have more than one woman and justify it on religious grounds.

Look at the Mormons. Look at the Muslims. I have a friend from Nigeria who is a Yoruba priestess. She told me about her cousin who had his parents arrange a marriage for him according to their tribal customs, even though he already had one wife over here. "Now you are not going to tell me that your traditions are superior to their traditions, are you?" she exclaimed. "That's cultural imperialism! That's how the white man took over Africa in the first place!"

We will try all kinds of intellectual games to dress up the

demon of lust in garments of respectability. We rationalize our actions by making statements like "you can't miss what you can't measure" or "if it's good to you, it's got to be good for you." We listen to songs that tell us "I don't see nothing wrong with a little bump and grind" and "If lovin' you is wrong, I don't wanna be right." Songs like "I'll make love to you, like you want me to, and I'll hold you tight, baby, all through the night" and "You just keep telling me this, telling me that once I've been with you you'll never go back. You say there's a lesson that you want to teach, well here I am baby, practice what you preach."[5] That song was number one on the charts for six straight weeks and then went double platinum!

We will dress up the demon of lust and pamper him to make him look respectable. And before those of you who are middle-aged get too holy and start coming down on this generation and their music too hard, let me take you back just a little bit so we will not get amnesia. Do you remember, "If you want a do right, all day's woman, you've got to be a do right, all night man" or "Let me hold you tight, if only for one night. Let me keep you near to ease away your fears?"[6]

You see, people dress the demon of lust up in beautiful clothes with sweet sounds and perfume and call it cultural. But the problem is not intellectual or cultural. The problem is spiritual. We have a spiritual problem when wrestling with the demon of lust. We do not need more information. We need more consecration. We do not need more happiness.

What we need is more holiness. The apostle Paul says to us "I beseech you, therefore, my brothers and my sisters, by the mercies of God that you present your bodies as a living sacrifice, holy and acceptable unto God."[7] We are busy trying to become socially acceptable and culturally acceptable, but we need to be acceptable unto God. "Let the words of my mouth and the meditation of my heart be acceptable unto Thee, Oh Lord, my Strength and my Redeemer."[8] What am I thinking about? What is on my mind? What are the meditations of my heart? "As a man or a woman thinketh in his or her heart, so are they."[9] Lord, I need you to get on the inside and clean up my heart.

"Create in me a clean heart, oh God, and renew a right spirit within me."[10] Those were David's words after coming face to face with his demon of lust. He knew he had a problem that was spiritual. It was not intellectual and it was not cultural. He did not need more information. He already had enough information. He knew that Bathsheba was married to somebody else. He knew that she was the wife of Uriah the Hittite. She was fine, yes, but she was off limits. "But not to the kid!," David reasoned. So he had Uriah killed so that he could marry his widow.[11] David had a spiritual problem, which later caused the remorseful leader to pray, "Cast me not away from thy presence and take not thy Holy Spirit from me."[12] Some of us wrestle night and day with this demon of lust, and that is just one demon! But Mary lived with seven!

Wrestling with the Demon of Doubt

Some of us are fighting the demon of doubt. We try to have faith and we want to believe. We would love to be able to trust again, but the demon of doubt keeps us pinned to the mat of maybe. Well, maybe it is not true. Maybe she is seeing somebody else, or maybe you are not supposed to be happy, or maybe you are not going to ever have anybody, or maybe you have been praying to the wrong God, or maybe there is not anything to this religious business anyway, or maybe Tina Turner was right when she asked "What's love got to do with it?"[13] Or maybe it is true that all men are dogs and can not be trusted, or maybe I have been wasting my time fooling around with black men or black women. Maybe I was just meant to be by myself. After all, I can be miserable all by myself. Or maybe I am not as smart as other people. Maybe I should not try to go to school. Maybe I just ought to give in. Maybe I just ought to give up. Maybe what all my friends are saying is right. Maybe what my enemies are saying is right. Maybe my mama was right when she said I was not anything, have not ever been anything, and will not ever amount to anything.

We doubt ourselves, we doubt others, and we doubt God. We doubt God's word. The demon of doubt whips us day and night. Every time we think we have taken one step forward, doubt comes along and kicks us back three.

Battling the Demon of Defeatism

Some of us are struggling against the demon of defeatism. We are defeated before we start. This demon tells us we can not do this, we can not do that, and we are not ever going to change. It is no use. If you are fat, you are fat. Forget the diet, you are not ever going to lose that weight. You can not go to school. You can not go to college. You can not make it through graduate school. You can not beat that cancer. You can not put a child through college. You can not tithe. You can not think and you can not read. And even if you could read, you could not remember. You can not get a worthwhile job. You can not have a decent relationship or a happy home. You made your bed, now lie in it. Some of us are struggling against the demon of defeatism!

Battling the Demon of Addiction

Others of us are getting whipped by the demon of addiction. That demon has us lying to ourselves, telling us we do not have a problem and that we can stop any time we want. It has us hiding whiskey from our family members, stealing money from our own mamas, and doing anything to feed our habit. We are getting whipped by the demon of addiction!

Battling the Demon of Denial

Some of us are living with the demon of denial. Our marriages are a living hell, but we place all of the blame upon our mates, insisting that we do not need counseling. Husbands in denial insist that their wives are the ones with the problem. When asked, "Why did you hit her?," they respond, "She kept on running her mouth, that's why. It's her fault. She brought it on herself." We are in denial!

Our kids are going to hell in a hand basket and we are blaming everybody except ourselves. We blame the schools and the teachers. We blame the television and the music. We blame their friends. "It is their peers, you know that peer pressure is something else," we say. We blame the church. "If the church was teaching what it should we would not have these problems. It is those hypocrite preachers who are not doing their job," we say. We blame the times. "Times have changed," we say. "Things are no longer the way they were when I was growing up. Today's kids have got a whole lot more pressure on them." We are in denial!

All too often, our kids are in the position they are in because we are in the position we are in! We are busy rearranging the deck furniture on the Titanic while the ship is going down! Somebody needs to tell our children there is no way to engage in safe sin. There is no sin that is safe. We are in deep denial. We live with the demon of denial.

The Demon of Low Self-Esteem

Others of us struggle with the demon of low self-esteem. After five hundred years of living in a culture of white supremacy, the demon of low self-esteem has a stranglehold on some of us. For some, it was the essence of a discussion we recently had in our men's Bible class and what the Association of Black Psychologists said a decade ago—that images of a white Jesus with blonde hair and blue eyes are not only historically inaccurate but also psychologically dangerous. Those images subtly say to Africans who are non-white, non-blonde, and non-blue-eyed that there is something wrong with them. These images subtly suggest that they are inferior, substandard, abnormal, or defective.

For others, it is a matter of not having "good hair." I took my wife and daughter out to dinner recently. Sitting next to us were two sisters talking about men with "good hair." In 1995! One said, "I don't like men with good hair. I like nappy hair." The other one replied, "Then just put a little water on it. It'll get crinkly." I did not know whether to scream or to vomit, especially with my young daughter sitting there and hearing that! I thought we had settled that one about thirty years ago. God did not make any hair that was not good hair. If it covers your head, it is good hair! In fact, my father, who is bald, puts it this way. He said, "God only made a few perfect heads and the rest he had to cover with hair."

We feed and reinforce the demon of low self-esteem with our conversations and our machinations of good hair and bad hair, and light skin and dark skin. The demon of low self-esteem has a stranglehold on some of us. You can still hear that old saying repeated in our communities—"If you're white, you're right, if you're yellow, you're mellow, if you're brown, hang around, but if you're black . . ."

For others like Mary, if you have been with more than one man or you have been passed around, picked over, and messed over, you begin to believe that you are not any good and nobody will ever really want you for you. You get to know this demon of low self-esteem on a first name basis.

Some of us battle the demon of lust. Some of us wrestle with the demon of doubt. Some of us fight with the demon of defeatism. Some of us box with the demon of addiction. Some of us arm-wrestle the demon of denial. And some of us are struggling with the demon of low self-esteem. Our waist is not small enough. Our breasts are not big enough. Our hair is not good enough. Our skin is not light enough. Our past is not clean enough. Our legs are not shapely enough. Our abs are not firm enough. Our job is not important enough. Our car is not "fresh" enough. Our home is not together enough. Our clothes are not stylish enough. We are not quite man or woman enough. That demon has a stranglehold on us!

A Living Hell

Some of us battle with one or two demons, but Mary had inside of her seven demons! Seven was the perfect number in the Jewish culture. It is made up of the human number four. Four seasons—winter, spring, summer, and fall. Four corners of the earth—north, east, south, and west. Four seasons of human life—childhood, the teenage years, adulthood, and old age. The human number four—Isaiah, Jeremiah, Ezekiel, and Daniel. Four—Matthew, Mark, Luke, and John.

Seven is the sum of the human number four and the God number three. Three—earth, ocean, and sky. Three—heaven, earth, and hell. Three—past, present, and future. Three—that which was, that which is, and that which is to come. Three men who showed up at Abraham's tent door in the heat of the day. Three—Peter, James, and John. Three—Father, Son, and Holy Ghost. Three crosses on Calvary against the Galilean sky. Three days in the grave and early on the third day, Jesus rose. Three is God's number. Seven is the sum of the human number four and the God number three. On the seventh day, the day after two times three, God rested. Seven denotes completion. Seven means perfection. So Mary, with seven devils in her, was therefore a perfect devil.[14]

Mary had seen it all. Mary had done it all. Mary had tried it all. People in the twelve-step program say that religion is for people who are afraid of going to hell, but spirituality is for people who already have been to hell. Mary had been to hell. Mary had lived in hell. Mary had hit rock bottom and she knew what the dregs of life tasted like.

A New Creature with a New Attitude

Oh, but Jesus made the difference. She was a new creation because of Jesus. When the Lord came into her life, all the old stuff passed away and everything about her life became new. Jesus made the difference.

You see when Jesus comes into your life, things change.

He changes the way you see things. In the Chinese language, the same symbol that is used to express crisis is also used to express opportunity. And that is how it is with the Lord in your life. Every time a crisis comes up, instead of seeing a crisis, you can see an opportunity. Instead of seeing a problem, you can see a possibility. Instead of seeing the end of the road, you can see a bend in the road. Instead of seeing doom and gloom, you can see a door through which God is getting ready to walk and a miracle that God is getting ready to work. He changes the way you see things. God also changes the way you see others. Before the Lord came into her life, Mary loved things and used people. But Jesus made the difference. He looked at her for who she was and what she could become, rather than what she was good for and what she could do for him, as most others did, and it changed her. She stopped loving things and using people. With the Lord in her life, she now loved people and used things.

Jesus changes the way you see others. You no longer look with the jaundiced eye of skepticism. You no longer look with the judgmental eye of "holier than thou." Instead, the Lord allows you to look with the Jesus eye, not of pessimism, but of optimism. Instead of the judgmental eye of "holier than thou," the Lord allows you to look with the Jesus eye of humility.

Jesus changes the way you see others, even your enemies—people who can not stand you, people who talk about you, and people you find it difficult to like. And let us be honest, there are some people who are extremely difficult to like.

They are evil, mean, and low-down. They lie, gossip, and have ugly attitudes. You hate to see them coming and when they live in your house, you hate to go home in the evening. They do not have anything nice to say about anybody. Some people are extremely difficult to like, but Jesus even changes the way you see them.

Let me tell you a story about my mentor, Dr. Samuel Proctor, who was Pastor Emeritus of Abyssinian Baptist Church in New York City and Professor Emeritus at Rutgers University. When lecturing to us in a doctoral program, Dr. Proctor once said he did not have any enemies on the face of the earth. His statement puzzled me because I knew a woman who could not stand the sight of Sam. I learned just how much she disliked him when I once mentioned Dr. Proctor's name to her during a casual conversation, and she went off on me. I wanted to know how he could say that he did not have an enemy in the world, knowing how much this woman disliked him. So I asked Dr. Proctor about her. He looked at me, smiled, and said, "Jeremiah, she is not my enemy. She is one of my confused friends." With the Lord in you, you see your enemies, people who can not stand you, people who talk about you, and people you find it difficult to like as your "confused friends." Does anybody out there have "confused friends"? I know I have got some.

Jesus changes the way you see things. Jesus changes the way you see others. If Mary had still been seeing things and people in the way she used to, she could not have moved openly, honestly, and lovingly around the countryside with the Lord. The "I knew you when" folks would have either run her away or driven her completely crazy, but Jesus made the difference.

And let me tell you something else. He not only changes the way you see things and changes the way you see others, but Jesus also changes the way you see yourself. First of all, Jesus helps you to see that you are a person of value and a person of worth. You are somebody and you are special simply because you are. You are made in the image of God. You are made as a precious part of creation. Your kinky hair, your broad hips, your oversized waist, your undersized breasts, your sable skin, your sketchy past, your skinny legs, your flabby abs, your low-paying job, your raggedy car, your junky house, your outdated clothes do not mean anything to the one who made you. God loves you and accepts you just as you are!

Jesus helps you to see yourself first as a person of value and a person of worth. Then he helps you to see yourself as a Christian under construction. You are not a finished product and I am not a finished product. We are under construction, we are in process, and we are constantly becoming. We are growing day by day. I am not what I used to be, I am not what I am going to be, but I also have enough sense and enough grace to know that I am not what I ought to be. I am a Christian under construction and God is not finished with me yet! I do not have to hold my head down when I make a mistake, because God has not yet perfected me. God is still preparing me.

Jesus changes the way you see yourself. First he helps you to see yourself as a person of worth, and then he helps you to see yourself as an unfinished product. But ultimately, he helps you to see yourself as somebody with a testimony that will bless somebody else's life. Can you imagine the lives that Mary touched as she told others what the Lord had brought her through, where the Lord had brought her from, and how the Lord had brought her out? Have you ever shared your testimony with another person who is struggling right now to cross over some terrain that you have already crossed over? Have you? You will be surprised how your testimony might help somebody.

There is one more thing that the Lord showed me in Mary's life and in my life. And if you look back at your life, you can probably see it, too. The Lord showed me that unless you have a test, you will never have a testimony. Mary had a testimony because of the tests she had been through. Some she failed and some she passed. Some you have failed and some you have passed. Some I failed and some I passed. But Jesus made the difference. He changed the way I see myself. Just because you failed in one thing does not mean you are a failure in all things. The Lord can change your negatives into positives. The Lord can change your tragedies into triumphs. The Lord can change your life into something beautiful. The Lord can take your mess and make a miracle!

Meditation and Prayer

Help, Lord! Help! Help! Sometimes I feel like I am going crazy. Spinning out of control! Losing my mind! But I am refreshed when I remember that you love and accept me just as I am—even on my crazy days!

Today, we ask you to evict that which attempts to make us crazy from our inward parts and begin the process of remolding our minds, hearts, and characters to reflect your divine purpose for us. Lead us beside still waters and restore our souls. We promise that we will cooperate, realizing that the changes you are working in us are for our good.

More Liberating Sermons

Are you an ordained minister with a sermon that is consistent with the tenor and spirit of those found in this book? I plan to edit and publish a second volume of *Women's Liberation: Jesus Style*. Perhaps you would like to join me in that project by submitting a copy of your sermon for consideration. Submissions may be in the form of a typewritten manuscript or audiotape. If selected, I have the right to publish your sermon but you will retain the copyright.

I am looking for sermons that clearly focus upon women's issues and concerns, and/or portray biblical women in a motivating light. Be sure to include your name, address, and telephone number so if your sermon is selected, I can contact you. For more information, or to send a submission, contact:

Stephanie F. Bibb
16781 Torrence Avenue, #208
Lansing, Illinois 60438

Notes

Chapter One: The Battle for Self-Esteem

1. Both groups adhered to Mosaic law. The source of enmity between them was a dispute concerning the correct place of worship. See Gail R. O'Day, "John," *The Women's Bible Commentary*, eds. Carol Newsom and Sharon H. Ringe (Louisville: Westminster/John Knox Press, 1992) p. 295.

2. This warning from God to the Israelites is expressed in Exodus 34:15-16 and Deuteronomy 7:3-4.

3. Robert T. Anderson, "Samaritans," *The Anchor Bible Dictionary*, vol. 5, ed. David Noel Freedman (New York: Doubleday, 1992) p. 941.

4. "Women," *The Anchor Bible Dictionary*, vol. 6, ed. David Noel Freedman (New York: Doubleday, 1992) pp. 953-954. The role of and attitude toward women in Old Testament Israelite culture was rooted in the demands of an agrarian economy, combined with a desire to perpetuate the family name. Childbearing was rewarded with security and prestige, while barrenness was viewed as a social disgrace and indication of God's disfavor.

5. Talmud *Tos Berakoth* 7:18; Bab Menahoth 43b, as referenced in John Temple Bristow's *What Paul Really Said About Women* (San Francisco: Harper & Row Publishers, 1988) p. 20.

6. See Leviticus 15:19-28 for a full explanation of the ritual of purification associated with menstruation.

7. Although the Samaritans adhered to Mosaic law, they held a different opinion concerning the proper place to worship from that of the Jews (John 4:20). Therefore, the Jews viewed the Samaritans as non-conformists and were unwilling to assume the ritual cleanliness of their women. The Jews felt the only safe practice was to assume a Samaritan woman was always unclean, hence a perpetual menstruator. For a full explanation, see C.K. Barrett, *The Gospel According to John: An Introduction with Commentary and Notes on the Greek Text* (London: S.P.C.K.,1955) pp. 194-195.

8. John 4:18, as paraphrased by the preacher.

9. John 4:13-14, as paraphrased by the preacher.

10. Ibid.

11. Ibid.

Chapter Two: Coping with Grief and Pain

1. John 19:26 KJV.

2. John 19:27 KJV.

3. The New National Baptist Hymnal (Nashville: National Baptist Publishing Board, 1977) p. 230.

Chapter Three: Building Relationships That Endure

1. The relationship between Abraham, Sarah, and Hagar is recounted in Genesis 16 and Genesis 21.

2. Genesis 19:1-11.

3. Genesis 37:1-36.

4. Joseph Scriven,"What A Friend We Have in Jesus," *The New National Baptist Hymnal* (Nashville: National Baptist Publishing Board, 1977) no. 340.

5. Matthew 12: 48—50 NIV.

6. Matthew 12:49 NIV.

7. For a full discussion of the concept of fictive kin, see Andrew Billingsley's *Climbing Jacob's Ladder: The Enduring Legacy of African American Families* (New York: Simon & Schuster, 1992) pp. 31-32.

8. Ruth 1:16-17 NRSV.

9. Shel Silverstein, *The Missing Piece* (New York: Harper-Collins, 1976).

10. Ruth 1:12-13,15, as paraphrased by the preacher.

11. John Fawcett, "Blest Be the Tie That Binds," *The New National Baptist Hymnal* (Nashville: National Baptist Publishing Board, 1977) no. 359.

12. Matthew 22:37.

13. Ruth 1:16-17, The New American Bible.

14. Ruth 1:16-17, as paraphrased by the preacher.

15. Dr. Maya Angelou, "The Black Family Reunion Pledge," *The Black Family Reunion Cookbook*, ed. The National Council of Negro Women (New York: Simon & Schuster) p. vi.

16. Ibid.

17. Ibid.

18. Matthew 19:26 NIV.

19. I Corinthians 6:20.

20. Taken from the Heidelberg Catechism, as referenced in *Space for God: The Study and Practice of Prayer and Spirituality* by Don Postema (Kalamazoo: CRC Publications, 1993) p. 35.

21. Romans 8:38-39, as paraphrased by the preacher.

Chapter Four: Never Ever Give Up

1. Lyrics from a popular rhythm and blues song recorded by Sam & Dave during the 1960s.

2. Matthew 15:24, as paraphrased by the preacher. It is important to understand that although Jesus came to the world to offer salvation and redemption to all, he unfolded his plan systematically, starting with the Jews, with whom the Old Covenant had been established.

3. Matthew 15:24.

4. Matthew 15:27.

5. Matthew 15:28.

6. Psalms 105:15 KJV.

7. A traditional hymn, frequently sung in African American churches. It was composed by Charles Wesley, an English hymn writer who lived between 1707 anf 1788.

8. Matthew 15:28, as paraphrased by the preacher.

9. Matthew 15:23, as paraphrased by the preacher.

10. This parable is recounted in Luke 18:1-8.

Chapter Seven: It's Time To Make A Change

1. Terry McMillan, *Waiting to Exhale* (New York: Viking Press, 1992).

2. Webster's Ninth New Collegiate Dictionary (Springfield: Merriam-Webster, 1993).

3. Matthew 7: 13-14, as paraphrased by the preacher.

4. For detailed information regarding the folklore connected with the Bethesda pool, see *The Interpreter's Bible*, ed. George A. Buttrick (New York: Abingdon-Cokesbury Press, 1952) vol. 8, p. 540.

5. Psalm 23:1, as paraphrased by the preacher.

6. John 10:10-12, as paraphrased by the preacher.

7. Joel 2:28.

8. Hebrews 12:1.

9. Acts 17:28.

10. The response given to this very important question is based upon I Thessalonians 5:23, Romans 8:37, and Jeremiah 29:11.

11. Romans 8:31.

12. Psalm 37:23 and Philippians 4:6.

13. Matthew 19:26 and Mark 11:23 reflect God's ability to do all things and move all barriers.

14. Romans 12:12.

15. John 6:63.

16. II Corinthians 5:7 and Hebrews 11:6.

17. Abraham and Sarah's faith journey is recorded in Genesis 12.

18. John 5:10.

Chapter Eight: Taming A Wild Woman

1. John 1:14.

2. Mark 5:28.

3. Mark 5:34 NRSV.

4. This miracle is recounted in Matthew 15:34-38.

5. Each of these are lyrics from popular songs recorded by R. Kelly, Luther Ingram, Boyz II Men, and Barry White respectively.

6. Lyrics from popular songs recorded by Aretha Franklin and Luther Vandross respectively.

7. Romans 12:1.

8. Psalm 19:14.

9. Proverbs 23:7.

10. Psalm 51:10 KJV.

11. This story is recounted in II Samuel 11:14-27.

12. Psalm 51:11 KJV.

13. The title of a popular song recorded by Tina Turner.

14. In this sentence, the author is using the word "devil" in a playful sense, much like us telling someone that they are a little "devil" or that they have "devilish" ways. He is not saying that Mary is a personification of the Evil One or a demon.

❧

Sources of Epigraphs

The Black Woman's Gumbo Ya-Ya: Quotations by Black Women, edited by Terri L. Jewell, (Freedom, CA: The Crossing Press, 1993), pp. 183, 157, & 195.

Proud Sisters: The Wisdom and Wit of African American Women, edited by Diane J. Johnson, (White Plains, NY: Peter Pauper Press, 1995), pp. 33 & 41.

Famous Black Quotations, edited by Janet Cheatam Bell, (New York: Warner Books, 1995), pp. 113 & 118.

The Quotations Home Page, http://www.lexmark.com/ data/ quote.html, copyright 1995 by Stephen L. Spanoudis.